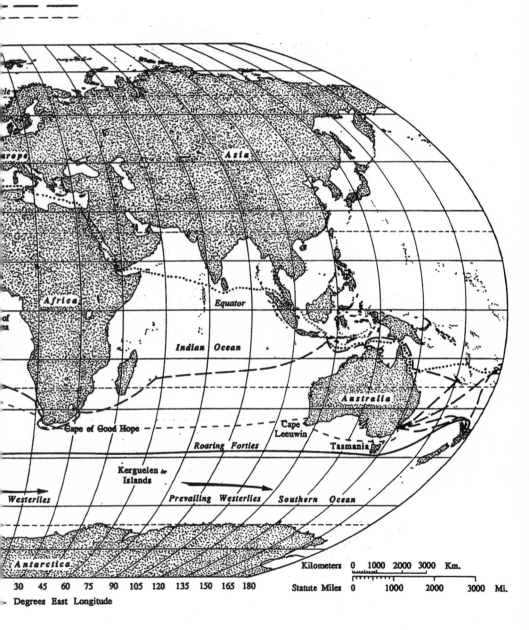

Asia

Europe

Africa

Equator

Indian Ocean

Cape of Good Hope

Cape Leeuwin

Australia

Tasmania

Roaring Forties

Kerguelen Islands

Westerlies

Prevailing Westerlies

Southern Ocean

Antarctica

| | 0 | 1000 | 2000 | 3000 | Km. |
| Kilometers | | | | | |

Statute Miles 0   1000   2000   3000   Mi.

30 45 60 75 90 105 120 135 150 165 180

Degrees East Longitude

RETURN TO THE SEA

Also by Webb Chiles

Storm Passage

The Open Boat

The Ocean Waits

A Single Wave

RETURN TO THE SEA

Webb Chiles

S

SHERIDAN HOUSE

Published 2004 by
Sheridan House Inc.
145 Palisade Street
Dobbs Ferry, NY 10522
www.sheridanhouse.com

Library of Congress Cataloging-in-Publication Data

Chiles, Webb.
     Return to the sea / Webb Chiles.
         p. cm.
     ISBN 1-57409-180-8 (alk. paper)
     1. Chiles, Webb—Travel. 2. Voyages around the world. I. Title.
     G530.C4774 A2 2004
     910.4'1—dc22   2004013073

ISBN 1-57409-180-8

Printed in the United States of America

To Carol
And the Last is First

Cafes sweet with the trilling of singing birds whose cages were full of mirrors to give them the illusion of company. The love songs of birds to companions they imagined which were only reflections of themselves.

—*Mountolive* by Lawrence Durrell

Be fair, or foul, or rain, or shine
The joys I have possess'd, in spite of fate, are mine.
Not Heaven itself upon the past has power.
But what has been, has been, and I have had my hour.

—Horace's Ode XXXIX as translated by John Dryden

He had seen men survive on ships who would have lost their reason and tranquility forever anywhere else. Course, wind, waves, position, the day's run, survival; out there only those words had meaning. Because it was true that real freedom, the only possible freedom, began five miles from the nearest coast.

—*The Nautical Chart* by Arturo Perez-Reverte

Between the vision
And the reality
Falls the Shadow

—my memory of "The Hollow Men" by T.S. Eliot

ACKNOWLEDGMENTS

With only a few exceptions—most notably when two decades ago I was falsely imprisoned as a spy in Saudi Arabia—people have treated me well during my voyages. One can almost count on the kindness of strangers.

I particularly want to acknowledge the hospitality shown to me at the Royal Cape Yacht Club in Cape Town, South Africa, and at the Fremantle Sailing Club in Fremantle, Australia.

It was a pleasure to spend time with Roberto Barros, yacht designer, sailor and kindred spirit, and his wife, Eileen, and their friends in Rio de Janeiro, Brazil.

Chris Stone and Elizabeth Bay Marina enabled me to enjoy Sydney, Australia, as much as I have in the past.

Hans Bernwall and the people at Scanmar Marine continue to provide personal service and support for their Monitor self-steering gear unusual in our consolidated times.

I want to thank Lothar Simon for again giving me the opportunity to publish a book; and Herb McCormick for putting a photograph of THE HAWKE OF TUONELA on the cover of *Cruising World*, which caused her to be recognized on five continents.

Parts of this book have previously appeared in somewhat different form in *Cruising World*; *SAIL*; and the *Fort Lauderdale Sun-Sentinel*.

CONTENTS

PART I

A LIFE FORGOTTEN

A Life Forgotten

I have already forgotten most of my life, which is just as well. Most lives are completely forgettable, and all mostly. Beethoven left us days, perhaps a week; Erik Satie an hour; Pachebel five or six minutes. Billions of others nothing more than their DNA. And for those of us without children not even that.

My life has been about three things: writing, sailing, and love. To fall into alliteration: words, wind, and women.

I have sailed around the world four times. I have married five women. And I have written more than a dozen books, some of which have even been published and occasionally read.

Sailing for me is not a pastime and boats are not merely beautiful toys, but survival capsules and an artist's tools. It probably does no harm to repeat something I wrote long ago: a sailor is an artist whose medium is the wind.

This is mostly the story of my fourth circumnavigation, which began and ended in Sydney, Australia.

Part of the first half of that voyage has been told in *A Single Wave*. While I don't want to repeat what I wrote there, some recapitulation is necessary for those who have not read that book.

Dangerously I will write from memory.

The danger is that, although I have been in many ways a statistical aberration, since my fifties my once excellent memory has been subject to the normal erosion of time. If there are differences between what I write now and what I wrote in *A Single Wave*, the earlier account, closer to the events, is factually accurate; but both are true.

I am curious to see if what I remember now is what I remembered then.

A Quick Half-Century

Snow, broken by dormers and chimneys on slanting roofs of red brick buildings, white beyond bare tree branches seen through the third story window of the Boston condominium where I am writing, for the moment ties worlds together.

Snow falling on the slopes of northern New Hampshire mountains from the windows of my friends' home where I stayed for several months after I sank RESURGAM.

Pushing snow with a broom from the deck of THE HAWKE OF TUONELA into Boston Harbor during the five years that Carol and I lived aboard at Constitution Marina.

Snow on low hills seen from a train rolling through southern Missouri in 1949, twisted limbs of other bare trees pencil black against pure white, on a journey that I only later learned was an attempt by my mother to escape reporters after my father's suicide on a slow news day in Saint Louis.

Snow and gray walls of water falling into the cockpit of EGREGIOUS as I approached Cape Horn in 1975.

I was born in Saint Louis in 1941, a few weeks before the Japanese attack on Pearl Harbor, and raised in one of those small brick suburban houses built for returning servicemen into which my mother and stepfather, and my mother's mother and my mother's stepfather, moved in 1946.

My mother and father separated before I was born.

From the time I was old enough to understand such things, I assumed that they had married only because she became pregnant. Decades passed before, while going through papers in a desk in a beach cottage I inherited after my grandmother's death, I came across a marriage license that showed they had married more than a year before my birth.

No one talked much in that small house. I do not know how any of them met, or separated, or stayed together. All of us were planets revolving around different suns. I was close only to my paternal grandmother and her last husband. Never divorced she outlived three husbands.

It is one of the curiosities of my life that I, who took the greatest risks, am the first man in my family to live past forty for several generations. At sixty-two I am venturing into the uncharted and unexpected waters of old age.

As an only child in such a house, and shy, which is not a crime—but seemed so at the time—it is not surprising that I became a solo sailor and a solitary writer. They are what I wanted to be since my early teens.

My fellow Missourian and transplanted New Englander, Samuel Clemens, said that all adventure begins with running away from home and with a book.

I physically ran away from home only once, and then for only a few hours, but my mind ran away all the time: in libraries and museums—the water lilies of Monet, the religious figures of Rouault, the tortured faces of Max Beckman—and later in music.

When I was fourteen my grandparents—and this to me always meant, Hazel, my father's mother, and Elmer, her last husband, for I had little to do with my mother's mother and her husband, though they lived in the other upstairs bedroom—retired and moved to a small beach house in San Diego, California. To everyone's relief—for they wanted me to be with them and I don't think the people in Missouri much did—I spent my summers there.

School was easy for me, but boring, and I was a good enough athlete to letter in a couple of sports; but I lived for those summers, for the day I could fly from land-locked Saint Louis and a few hours later be running across the beach and diving into a wave.

I spent most of each summer day on the beach and in the water. From the sand I watched sailboats move across the horizon. I did not know anyone who sailed. I had never sailed myself. But I knew that I would, just as I knew I would write.

That was in the late 1950s. I made my first attempt at Cape Horn in 1974. Fast forward twenty years.

I went to college and briefly to graduate school. I married twice, first to a fine woman who, we were too young to realize, wanted very different things from life than I did, then to the only real marital mistake I made.

I worked at unimportant and uninteresting jobs for eleven years. When I was twenty-five I bought my first boat in Berkeley, California, a 26-foot sloop. Eight months later the woman who was then a part of my life and I sailed it to San Diego.

I saved money. I read about other voyages. I wrote unpublished novels.

I sold the first boat and bought a 35-foot sloop, aboard which I lived, first with the woman I had sailed with from Berkeley, then, briefly, with my second wife, then alone. I read about the sea. I dreamed and imagined and I planned. Many failures, including war, are failures of the imagination, and I did not intend to fail.

During that period Francis Chichester made his well-publicized one-stop circumnavigation. It was obvious that someone would soon go around non-stop. Most of the interest was in Europe; I was in California and I knew I was not ready. I did not have the right boat or the money, and I had no talent for begging.

A "race" was arranged, if that is the word for what became a trial of endurance. Only Robin Knox-Johnson in the slowest boat finished, and another entrant, Donald Crowhurst, cowered in the South Atlantic and radioed false positions that caused others to believe for a while that he was leading the race before he committed suicide.

What is forgotten is that Nigel Tetley, who was actually leading the race, was forced to give up after making it almost back to England because he damaged his boat while pushing, believing he had to stay ahead of Crowhurst. A few years later, in obscurity, Tetley too committed suicide.

Three of the contestants in the race made it around Cape Horn alone: Knox-Johnson, Tetley, and Bernard Moitessier, who famously decided the exercise was meaningless and continued on to the South Pacific rather than return to Europe. And there had been Chichester a couple of years earlier.

But earlier books had turned my mind toward the Horn.

One of my favorites was *Alone in the Roaring Forties* by the first man to survive a solo rounding of the cape, the Argentinean Vito Dumas, who did so in the early 1940s. The Southern Ocean was empty then, even at the height of World War II.

And I knew of Al Hansen, who had rounded the Cape even earlier, going east to west, but he did not survive. The wreckage of his boat washed onto the coast of Chile.

In America no one had ever even attempted to sail alone for Cape Horn. I hoped that no one would before my five-year plan, initiated when I bought the 35-foot sloop in 1969, ended with my departure in 1974. I need not have worried.

A year before I was ready to go, rather than modify the sloop, I traded it in for a 37-foot stock boat that I thought would be a little faster and stronger. It could be set up from the beginning as a cutter, without an engine, and with other idiosyncratic preferences, including no lifelines, which I do not think are generally much use in keeping people on boats. I assumed nothing. I considered every detail. I deliberately sailed in such bad weather as Southern California could muster. I read. And I imagined. And in the end I pretty much got it right.

Setting the date and time of my departure a year in advance, I left my office for the last time at 6:00 p.m. on a Friday and raised sail and pushed away from the dock at Harbor Island Marina at 11:00 a.m. the following morning.

I had drawn out my retirement funds and had the boat and about $10,000. Everything I owned in the world was at risk, including my own life, and would continue to be for the next twenty years, during which I twice lost everything except my life.

Storm Passage tells the story of that voyage which resulted in a two-stop circumnavigation in what was then world record time, and, on December 12, 1975, my becoming the first American to pass Cape Horn alone.

When I sailed back into San Diego Bay at the end of that voyage, I did not call a press conference like some child jumping up and down, shouting, "Look at me! Look at me!" I cleared customs, tied the boat up, and took a cab to my grandmother's house, where she and Suzanne, whom I had met in New Zealand, were waiting.

I spent five months non-stop at sea on the first leg of the voyage, from San Diego south around the Horn and east in the Southern Ocean until forced to put into Auckland for repairs. It is a good line to say that after five months alone at sea I married the first woman I met, particularly since it is true.

Back in America, I quickly became restless. *Storm Passage* was published and I sold EGREGIOUS, the 37-foot cutter, and looked for another challenge, one that was qualitatively different.

Two years after returning in EGREGIOUS, I sailed from San Diego, going out between the breakwaters at the end of Mission Beach, where I had sat and dreamed as a boy, in CHIDIOCK TICH-BORNE, an 18-foot open boat.

Over the next four years I sailed that little yawl most of the way around the world, setting various records and having some adventures. In June of 1982 I went into Rabigh, Saudi Arabia to fit the spare rudder after bending the original on an uncharted coral reef in the Red Sea, and was locked up as a spy.

This happened only a few days after I had returned from California where my grandmother had died and Suzanne and I had separated. If you marry for any reason other than money, a divorce is a death, and only the ending of my second marriage did not cause me pain.

I was jailed for only two weeks, but I did not know what the duration would be at the time. Those days first in a cell in Rabigh Gaol and then in solitary confinement— which naturally I preferred—at the police headquarters a hundred miles south in Jeddah were the darkest of my life.

When I was released, as inexplicably as I had been arrested, I was expelled from the country, while my boat remained behind, and I flew back to California.

The story of those four years is told in *The Open Boat: Across the Pacific* and *The Ocean Waits*.

The following year the builders of CHIDIOCK TICHBORNE, a stock Drascombe Lugger, shipped a sistership to Egypt for me. I sailed it part way back down the Red Sea to pick up my earlier track, then through the Suez Canal and the Mediterranean, with one stop in Malta, to the marina in Vilamoura, Portugal, and on to the Canary Islands, where she was capsized on a mooring while I was not aboard.

While I admired the little boat as much as any I have owned, she was too small to be my permanent home. I sold my grandmother's house and used part of the money to buy a 36-foot Olin Stephens-designed sloop in England, which I named RESURGAM in a gesture of hope that my life would rise again.

I had both boats in Vilamoura at the same time in the fall of 1983. On Christmas Day, when we were invited to the same party in the marina, I met Jill, who became my next wife and sailed most of my next circumnavigation with me in RESURGAM.

The voyage was a conventional one. My days of setting records were behind me, though my days of living at the edge of human experience were not.

We sailed west 1½ times around the world, twice transiting the Panama Canal and twice spending a year in Sydney, Australia.

Jill enjoyed the sea and sailing, but ours was never a settled relationship, and we separated and came back together several times.

We were apart when in 1984 I completed my second circumnavigation at Nuku Hiva in the Marquesas Islands after making a solo passage from Panama.

We were together when I completed my third circumnavigation at Nuku Hiva six years later.

And we were together when RESURGAM sailed out Sydney Heads and headed east across the Tasman in September 1991.

3 *Starting a Circle*

I left Sydney with regret. It was my favorite city in the world, and still is, though now in a tie with Cape Town.

The harbor may be the greatest in the world, all hills and scalloped coves, which the confluence of several small rivers has carved from sandstone. While there is no great single concentration of boats, each of those coves is filled with moorings. From the one we had rented in Elizabeth Bay, a little more than a mile east of the Opera House and the city center, there were always boats and ships and ferries to watch. On weekends the harbor exploded with activity, with several races taking place simultaneously using buoys and islands as marks.

Despite the hills and tall buildings Sydney is a horizontal city, in contrast to San Francisco whose hills are higher, if not steeper, and where the eye moves vertically.

Sydney's bands of color begin with the gray-green or blue of the harbor, depending on the proportion of cloud and sun; then the green of equally high hills, all rising about 100 feet, covered with white red-roofed buildings; above them a vast band of usually blue sky; all leading the eye inland toward the Opera House and the Harbor Bridge.

It was an easy city in which to live. Climbing up the hill from Elizabeth Bay to shop, or up to Potts Point, then down 110 steps to Woolloomooloo, up to the Domain and Botanical Gardens whose trees are filled with screeching cockatoos, then down to Farm Cove and the Opera House on our way downtown or to catch a ferry.

After months in South Pacific islands, we enjoyed having access to book and music stores, to movies and chandleries.

I had written a novel during the year we spent there, I was happy and I had hope.

As RESURGAM moved out into the Tasman Sea, the city quickly disappeared behind the headlands. While I have liked many places in the world, I could only remember leaving with such regret once before, and that was New Zealand after I spent a few months recovering with Suzanne at Cook's Beach following being adrift for two weeks in the South Pacific when CHIDIOCK TICHBORNE capsized. I looked back and wondered if I would ever see Sydney again. I did not know that I had just begun another circumnavigation.

The Tasman has a deserved reputation for being a rough sea. During my first circumnavigation, I entered it after spending three months south of 40°S only to run into a March cyclone, but this time we were able to pick our weather and crossed uneventfully, stopping for a week at Lord Howe Island.

Lord Howe is one of the most beautiful islands in the world. Only five or six miles long and with a population of between two and three hundred, a turquoise lagoon on the west bordered by a reef and tall Norfolk pines, green hills at the north, and a sheer sided mountain at the south rising 2,000 feet straight up from the sea, Lord Howe is a legitimate version of paradise, which makes its small war memorial all the more incongruous and moving.

I had noticed these memorials all through the South Pacific, from Tahiti to Tonga to Fiji to Lord Howe, as well, of course, in New Zealand and mainland Australia. But the islands seemed impossibly remote from Northern Hemisphere power struggles, particularly in 1914-18 when Europe and the carnage in the fields of Flanders were months away by ship, not twenty-four hours away by plane or immediately observed by satellite television.

Like all the others the memorial on Lord Howe had been built for *The Great War*, and then added to for World War II, and again for Korea and Vietnam. From the inscribed names, one family on Lord Howe had a man killed in each of those wars.

In New Zealand I celebrated my fiftieth birthday by buying

a handheld GPS. The system was not officially operational, but all the satellites were up and the price of receivers dropped below $2,000, so I splurged. I also did all the other tasks and bought all the equipment on the permanent running list I keep. After all, if not at 50, then when?

In January 1992 we sailed east for Cape Horn. Our reluctant plan was to return to the East Coast of the United States where we would remain for three or four years to bring what might laughingly be called our capital up to a level sufficient to sail away again permanently. The plan was reluctant because I no longer liked having a boat in America, or Europe either for that matter, both of which are too crowded, too expensive, and too regulated.

I was hoping that the novel I had written in Sydney would bring in enough money to make the return unnecessary. Even if it did we both wanted to sail for Cape Horn, Jill, who was always adventurous, to become a Cape Horner, I drawn back to the great reaching winds of the Southern Ocean and the scene of perhaps the defining moment of my life. Navigating with a sextant in 1975, cloudy skies had forced me to sail well south of Horn Island; this time I wanted to see the rock, and I put the waypoint in the GPS before we left New Zealand.

Landlocked dreamers looking at atlases and PR types championing round the world races have perpetuated a myth of great waves roiling unchecked by any land mass around the globe south of 40°S. As those of us who have actually been there and are not addicted to hyperbole know, waves rise and fall in the Southern Ocean with specific pressure gradients, just as they do on every other body of water. In December 1975 I had twenty- to thirty-foot breaking waves and Force 12 wind off Cape Horn, and a day or two later and a couple of hundred miles due east, I sat becalmed on glassy water, watching an albatross swim a slow circle around the boat. In 1992, we found that you can't even count on the wind blowing from the west.

Less than a thousand miles out from New Zealand the wind headed us. Our belief that this was a temporary aberration in a region famous for its strong and persistent westerlies was soon replaced by dismay, frustration, and finally weary resignation. For forty-one of the fifty-eight days we spent at sea between New Zealand and Punta del Este, Uruguay, the wind blew from the direction we wanted to go, east until we reached the Horn and north when we made the turn.

Only for one week as we approached Cape Horn did we experience the fine reaching conditions I had remembered and longed for.

On all but the worst days when heavy water poured over the deck as RESURGAM pounded to windward and leapt off waves, I put on my foulweather gear in the afternoon and spent an hour or two in the cockpit.

One afternoon an albatross glided down and hung beside us. He turned his head toward me. Eye met eye. Life acknowledged life amidst desolate mountains of water, until with an almost imperceptible curvature of one wing, he arched away and was gone.

The day of the Horn was clear and cold and calm. The mountains of Tierra del Fuego turned purple beyond a glassy sea in the first light of dawn. Lumpy seas rose as we passed onto the continental shelf and depths decreased from thousands of feet to a hundred. With too little wind, we powered to keep from being tossed about uncontrollably. Near noon a few miles off Horn Island, a line of clouds with rain drifted down on us, obscuring visibility and bringing with them the north wind that would dog us, mixed with calms, as we worked our way up the east coast of South America toward Uruguay.

The contrast with my first rounding of the great cape in 1975 in hurricane force winds, tied in the cockpit, steering down thirty-foot breaking waves, EGREGIOUS making eight knots under bare poles, a rooster tail shooting up from her stern, could not have been greater. No one else has dared to say it, but some days Cape Horn is just another place.

Fortunately we arrived in Punta del Este in mid-March, which is the end of their summer season. In season Punta is the playground for the South American rich, particularly Argentineans, a Martha's Vineyard South, and prices are high and the harbor is packed. Everyone had gone home the weekend before we sailed across the hundred-mile wide mouth of the River Platte. Summer houses stood deserted; prices were reasonable; and we were able to find space behind the breakwater after one night bouncing at anchor in dangerously shallow water assaulted by the wind known as a pampero.

Two images remain of Uruguay. The first is a sculpture of a hand rising, finger partly flexed, from a beach in Punta del Este, as though a giant is buried beneath the sand and reaching for the sun and help.

The second was in Montevideo, to which we had gone by bus to obtain visas from the Brazilian Embassy. In late afternoon we walked along the promenade beside the harbor. We passed two couples sitting on benches partially sheltered by the seawall. Only a few feet apart, they were oblivious to one another. The first couple were young lovers. The second, dressed in black, were a middle-aged man and an old woman. The woman, whom we assumed to be the man's mother, was crying. They seemed to have just come from a funeral. The couples were the same: a man with his arms around a woman, her face buried against his chest: the embraces of love and death identical.

A few weeks in Uruguay, a longer than expected stay in Rio de Janeiro because Jill required medical treatment and where I received a letter that my literary agent felt he had exhausted the possible publishers for the novel I had written in Sydney, an easy passage around the bulge of Brazil to the Virgin Islands, a brush with a freighter off Puerto Rico on the way to Florida via the Old Bahamas Channel, a week in Key West, a few days in Fort Lauderdale, and Jill left and I sailed offshore, opened the seacocks, and as RESURGAM's bow dipped below the waves for the last time and her stern raised, I stepped into the warm water of the Gulf Stream.

Twenty-six hours later and more than a hundred miles north, I half climbed and was half pulled by two confused, sleepy fishermen into a boat anchored off Sebastian Inlet.

I have told the full story of those twenty-six hours in *A Single*

Wave and I don't want to retell them or relive them even in my mind again.

I will say that they were not hours of terror, but of cosmic calm. In the first few minutes I took off my wristwatch and let it sink. Hours, minutes no longer had meaning for me. I was beyond time.

Even friends have said that I changed my mind. But I never did and never have. When after floating effortlessly for perhaps nine hours waiting for a death that apparently overslept that morning, I began to swim toward the land by then more than ten miles to the west, it was not a decision of the mind, but of the body. I felt something pluck at my leg, looked down into the clear water and saw a tiny fish taking a tentative nibble, said aloud, "Not yet" and, without thinking, started to swim.

Twice in my life I have suffered terrible thirst. When I was adrift for two weeks in the inflatable dinghy after CHIDIOCK TICHBORNE pitchpoled in the South Pacific, I lived on six sips of water a day. During those twenty-six hours in the Atlantic off Florida, the salt water soon began to cut into my eyes and mouth like a knife. The body needs water, sleep, and food in that order, and food is a distant third. Those two periods of thirst, ten years apart and now ten and twenty years past, burned themselves indelibly into every cell of my body. I can feel them now, at this very moment.

Two Days

As water streamed from me, running down my face and chest to my legs and feet onto the rough deck in a reluctant release, words streamed from the two fishermen.

"Where did you come from?"

"How long have you been in the water?"

"Are you all right?"

"What happened to your boat?"

The boat is real, I thought through waves of exhaustion. I felt as though I were underwater, looking up at a world of sunlight playing on the surface several feet above me. I saw two men, both around thirty, one almost as tall as I was but heavier with the beginning of a belly and long blond hair tied back in a pony tail, the other shorter and with short dark hair. Both were staring at me in astonishment, as though I had fallen from another planet. The boat is real, I thought again. I could feel the stern rail digging into my hip. I was Lazarus brought back to life reluctantly, slightly surprised and curious that the earth in my mouth was real, though it would be months before I thought of such allusions. At that moment and for some time to come only the present and the next single step mattered.

"Thank you," I said, listening to my voice as I had when I first spoke in Auckland after five months at sea on the first passage around the Horn. "I don't know how much longer I could have lasted." The words hurt. My throat hurt. "Could I have some water?"

"Sure."

"Of course."

"The galley's forward. We can make coffee. Or there's beer. Or soda. Cold. In the freezer."

"Water would be . . ." My voice failed. I pushed myself away from the stern. In the ocean I had moved easily, but now each action required specific direction. My own body was as foreign, as strange as the external world.

I had to tell my hands to reach back and push away from the stern and I had to look down and watch to be certain they did. My body tilted forward. Too late I told my left leg and foot to move and I started to fall. One of the men grabbed my arm.

"Can you walk?"

"Just sit on the deck. I'll bring it to you."

"I think I can make it," I croaked. A large, white, waist-high box was a few feet away. I have been through this before, I thought, as I tottered forward. I reached the box and hung on. One of the men came back with a gallon water container.

"Bring him a glass."

"You want a glass? I thought you could just keep this."

"I don't need a glass." I tried to smile as I took the jug, but I knew the expression probably came out as a grimace. The jug was solid and heavy in my hands. My fingers clumsily grasped the handle. I lifted the container to my face and took a small, tentative sip, still watching myself, still separated from my body. For a moment the water hurt my lips, then it soothed. I swished it around my mouth, which was so filled with salt that the first sip was brackish. Swallowing hurt. Smiling hurt. I felt the water go down, reach my stomach, and wondered what would happen. My stomach lurched, then settled. I took a second small sip. This was better. The impulse to upend the bottle and gulp was strong, but I only took a third small sip, which was wonderful. The tense dying animal relaxed.

Lowering the bottle, I managed to say, "My name is Webb Chiles. Where are we?"

"About eight miles off Sebastian Inlet."

"Where's that?"

"North of Fort Pierce. I'm Luke. This is my brother Jimmy."

The bigger man offered his hand and I shifted the water container. The handshake hurt, and Luke released me quickly. All three of us looked down at my hand. The skin was blanched and spongy. "Sorry," Luke said. Jimmy made a vague waving gesture rather than try to shake hands.

"I was asleep when you called. I thought I was dreaming, dreaming that I heard someone call. I sort of woke not knowing where I was, and when I remembered we were way out from the shore I knew I had to be dreaming and was already back asleep when I heard you call again."

"North of Fort Pierce?" Jill and I had driven a rental car down to Key West a few years earlier when we had flown back from Portugal to see her parents. "That's near Daytona Beach?"

"Close. Sebastian's about halfway between Daytona and Fort Pierce."

I took another small sip of water and was silent while I tried to understand. We had stopped for lunch in Daytona Beach and then returned to the Interstate. I seemed to remember driving two or three hours before we reached Fort Lauderdale. I had known that the Gulf Stream was carrying me north. I had thought I had drifted to West Palm or perhaps a little north of that. Twenty or thirty miles. "I'm thinking a little slowly. How far are we from Fort Lauderdale?"

Jimmy's voice was excited. "You did say Fort Lauderdale." He turned toward his brother. "I told you he said Fort Lauderdale." Then back to me. "It's all of 125 miles. Maybe 135. Did your boat go down there? What happened? What kind of boat?"

One hundred and twenty-five miles? Maybe more? I pictured the Florida chart from the curve of the Keys to the turn at Elbow Reef, fairly straight due north to Miami and Fort Lauderdale, then tending west of north, coming back east at Cape Canaveral. One hundred and twenty five miles was a five-knot average for twenty-four hours. Not a bad day's run on most sailboats. I had sailed straight out from Fort Lauderdale, due east. The wind was light. I could still see the lights of the apartment towers beside the harbor entrance an hour before RESURGAM sank.

I noticed that the sky was lightening. I glanced at my wrist. The watch was gone. I remembered dropping it, watching it drift down, being beyond time. And I thought of RESURGAM on the ocean bed. The thought brought pain. "What time is it?"

"5:30. Almost. When did your boat sink?"

"Yesterday. 3:00 a.m."

"You've been in the water twenty-six hours?"

"I guess." I looked past them to the eastern sky and said aloud but mostly to myself. "I was getting tired. I don't know how much longer I would have lasted. But I would have made it to dawn.

"I almost reached another fishing boat a few hours ago, but it moved away without hearing me. I knew I wouldn't make the shore, so all I was doing was trying to last until dawn and maybe someone would see me. I wasn't even sure you were real, not a hallucination."

"That's some swim." The two brothers spoke simultaneously.

The box I was leaning against covered the engine, which I could feel vibrating beneath me. I was cold and the warmth was welcome. "Why isn't anyone steering?" I suddenly thought and asked.

"We're anchored. We anchored to sleep."

"In how much water?"

"About 180 feet. We're after tilefish. Been out a couple of days and needed sleep. Thought we'd start again about now."

My legs were weakening and I slid down the side of the engine box until I was sitting on the deck. "Sorry. I can't stand any longer." I took another sip of water. "My boat sank in about a thousand feet."

"You must have thought you were going to die for sure."

"Yes. That is what I thought."

Luke and Jimmy stood looking down at me, beginning to imagine themselves in my place. We were all quiet for several seconds, before Luke said, "I'll call the Coast Guard," and moved from my field of vision. I heard the static as the radio switched on, then, "Coast Guard Fort Pierce. Coast Guard Fort Pierce. This is the PROWLER. Come in."

A few seconds later a voice answered, but I lost the words when Jimmy asked, "Do you want some food or anything."

"I don't think I could eat."

"Something else to drink? Coffee?"

I was cold. "Maybe coffee."

Jimmy smiled, glad to be able to do something. "I'll boil the water." As he started forward, he added, "There's a shower, nothing fancy, plenty of hot water, if you want to get the salt off."

"That's worth trying to stand for," I said.

A half hour later I sat again, leaning against the engine box, dressed now in an old gray T-shirt and clean but paint splattered and faded yellow baggy shorts that Jimmy found for me. The shorts and T-shirt I had worn in the water lay spread across the top of the box. I was still unshaven. Jimmy had offered me a razor, but when I tried to use it, my skin was too tender.

The engine thrummed cyclically beneath me, driving the PROWLER south at twelve knots, thrusting through small waves. The flat brown shore was visible in bright sunshine a few miles to the west. Despite the shower and dry clothes and coffee, I was cold. The heat from the engine felt good, but it did not penetrate far enough. Although the ocean had been warm, more than 80°F, it had lowered my body temperature; and I would be cold deep inside for several more days.

I sipped from my second bottle of Coke. Liquid stayed down. I had even nibbled at the center of a slice of white bread. Although my body wanted warmth, my mouth and throat welcomed cool liquid.

In the pocket of the shorts was my billfold. It was made of elephant skin, purchased legally in South Africa where the elephant population of Kruger National Park must be culled. Elephants get wet and the billfold was in better shape than I was. The credit cards were still inside, as was about $100 in damp bills. Even my driver's license was readable.

They were taking me to Fort Pierce. The Coast Guard had offered to come out and I had told Luke and Jimmy that I did not want to cause them to lose time fishing, but Luke said he had been thinking of going back in that morning anyway, the fishing being poor. Automatically I looked down again to see what time it was, and found again only a red, sunburned band around my wrist. Another, smaller sunburned band was on my ring finger. I was passive cargo being carried back to the world, back to life. But there is nothing for me there, I thought. Everything is gone. I would get a hotel room and go to sleep. I couldn't think beyond that. It was enough for the present just to have something to drink and not be in pain.

A change in engine sound woke me. My back was warm, but my feet were cold and my body had stiffened. Awkwardly I pulled myself upright and saw the breakwater. Jimmy was at the wheel, his back to me, but Luke was aft, beyond the overhang of the cabin, and shouted above the diesel, "We'll be at the Coast Guard dock in a few minutes."

I shuffled toward the stern. The glare of the sun hit my eyes and I realized I did not have any glasses. I would not be able to drive a car. This was Sunday. Tomorrow I could get a new prescription. I did not like to ask, but I said to Luke, "Do you have any old shoes or flip-flops I can wear? Just until I can buy something."

"Sure. Sorry. I should have thought of it." He turned and rummaged in a locker and came out with a pair of white knee high rubber boots. "I thought there was something else."

"Those will do. Write down your address and I'll send them back to you. I want to pay you for your lost time and the fuel too."

Luke hesitated before saying, "I couldn't take money for saving a man's life."

"It's not for that, but there's no need for you to have to pay for the privilege. You must be using a lot of diesel and you'll lose the day fishing."

"Well . . . whatever you want."

"I've got about a hundred or so on me, but somewhat wet. If there's a cash machine somewhere ashore, I can get more."

"O.K. For the fuel and Jimmy anyway."

The boat slowed as we headed up the channel. A few other power boats and sailboats passed us, heading out.

I looked at the shore. On each side of the breakwater low waves broke, then the PROWLER was through the gap in the beach, lines of houses on either side. And the land enclosed me.

Two years to the day later.

Her ad in the Key West yellow pages under the heading, Notaries Public, was too cute. It read: "Alice's Wonderland Weddings. Your place or mine." And so we called several of the other listed notaries without success before resorting to her. In the Monroe County Courthouse at the end of Highway One, we had learned that in Florida weddings are performed by notaries. All you need is a license which in 1994 cost $84. No blood test. No waiting period. No witnesses. And, at least in Key West as the woman behind the counter joked, not even any identification.

We paid for the license and went back out into the hot summer sun.

"You call," Carol said.

As I feared, the telephone was answered by a chirpy, "Alice in Wonderland." Nevertheless three days later we found ourselves sitting nervously on a white cane sofa on the second story balcony of Alice's pastel blue, turquoise trimmed clapboard house in Old Town, while Alice, whose real name is Ida, filled out a form. She just used "Alice" to be listed first in the yellow pages, she explained.

The balcony was a jungle. Potted plants hung perilously close above us, while others grew voluptuously from urns on the floor and vines clung to railings and roof supports.

Ida was about my age, I guessed. She was a short fat woman with a strong New York accent. She was wearing a floral print muumuu and brown leather sandals. I am nervous, I thought, which is odd after all the times I've done this. No. Not odd. The importance never diminished. If anything, it became greater as I grew older.

In the window behind Carol I saw our reflections and reached to take her hand. Both our palms were moist beyond the tropical heat. She smiled at me, and I felt myself grinning back. "You look beautiful. Stunning." I said. This was, I realized, the first time I had seen her wearing makeup and jewelry and high heels.

Other than the T-shirts and other Duval Street merchandise purveyed to tourists, Key West is not a good place to shop. Permanent residents still tend to drive to mainland malls, and we had been fortunate to find Carol's cream colored sandals and off white linen dress at Chissum's. I wore a short-sleeve white cotton shirt bought for the occasion and tan slacks and Docksiders, my only pair of shoes.

She was in her mid-thirties, almost twenty years younger than I was, and she looked even younger than she was. Her brown hair had been lightened to blond by the sun. Both of us were deeply tanned.

"There," Ida/Alice said, turning from the white wrought iron coffee table on which she had been writing. "The state's work is done. You two are so comfortable with one another. You must have been together a long time."

We had known each other for two months.

5 Two Years

After a few days I flew from Florida to New England to spend a week with my friends, Bill and Hemmie Gilmore, in their house on a hill in northern New Hampshire overlooking the White Mountains. I ended up staying five months. Their kindness was limitless.

Most of the time I was in their home, they were away, sailing across the Atlantic from Spain to the Caribbean.

Not long after their return, an offer to make a lecture tour along the East Coast took me to Boston and left me in Miami.

I rented a car and drove to Key West, where I rented a tiny room and sat on the beach and looked at the turquoise water and my memories.

Two months of that was more than enough. I found myself wanting a boat, however small, as a space of my own, a home; so I delivered a car to New York to look at one that seemed promising in Connecticut. I didn't buy it, but I kept looking and in June found a 37-foot sloop named HAWKE in a boatyard on the Vermont shore of Lake Champlain. Of the same vintage as RESURGAM, a mid-70s former racer, she was bigger, rougher, and beaten up; but I thought she was basically sound, would sail well, and could be improved. Besides she was all I could afford.

I powered her through the Champlain Canal and down the Hudson River to New York City.

Before the onset of winter, I sailed south to the Florida Keys, where a letter came from a German physician, asking if I would be interested in sailing him and a friend and his 44-foot Peterson cutter from Boston to Lisbon the following summer. I never knew how he got my name or address. I was not in the delivery business; but I had nothing else to do and needed the money, so I accepted.

His friend was Carol, and between us it was love at first sight, even though that sight was at a loading zone at Boston's Logan Airport, which is perhaps the ugliest and most chaotic in the world. The words "love" and "Logan" are seldom used in the same sentence.

I admire people who take risks, who have the nerve to leap into the unknown. Carol, who otherwise led a fairly normal life—raised in Charlotte, North Carolina in a family of four children, college there, graduate school at Harvard—had taken one leap in a six-month leave of absence from her architectural career and took a much bigger one by marrying me. You meet a lot of people and sometimes you meet the right one at the right time.

We met in June, were married in August, and in December when Carol's leave of absence came to an end drove to Boston, where we rented the downstairs of a house in Belmont, not far from her office in Harvard Square.

The following April I flew back to Florida, re-commissioned HAWKE, now renamed THE HAWKE OF TUONELA, after a piece of music by Jean Sibelius called "The Swan of Tuonela," and sailed her north.

That winter I worked with frozen fingers rebuilding her interior while she sat snow covered in a slip at Constitution Marina. I put liner on the overhead and the insides of the hull, bookshelves and some cabinets over the upper berths in the main cabin and beside the quarter berths aft, turned the open sail storage space forward into a V-berth, moved the head, replaced the stove and the cabin sole, rewired lights, and generally transformed a stripped out racer into something more livable.

We moved aboard full-time the following April.

6 Four Seasons

Completing my fourth circumnavigation, sailing south and east to Sydney, became an arbitrary goal. I missed Sydney and the Southern Hemisphere. While Boston is in many ways an interesting city, its life is indoors, in classrooms and libraries and laboratories and concert halls, and for me the climate was intolerable. It was also the true test that I had put my life back together; I needed the open horizon and the purity of the rhythms of ocean passages.

To my surprise, because as an architect she is a round peg in a round hole, Carol decided she wanted to sail with me. We made a five-year plan to save money and prepare the boat with departure set for June 2001, just as I had once made a five-year plan to sail from San Diego in 1974.

Until then we lived a Boston Harbor version of The Four Seasons.

Fall

Most bicycles disappear from the rack.

The summer people disappear too. Those of us who are left on the year round lived-in fifty boats at Constitution Marina are like the residents of any beach resort after Labor Day. Among the mostly familiar faces are a few newcomers, anxiously awaiting their first winter aboard.

The marina is tucked away in the northwest corner of Boston's inner harbor and in the center of history. The Freedom Trail runs outside our front gate and we float where British

Letting some fresh, cold air into THE HAWKE OF TUONELA *at Constitution Marina. One of five Boston winters*

troops landed to begin the assault on Bunker Hill. Spearing the sky to the north is the obelisk monument to that battle. A quarter mile away stands Bunker Hill Community College of "Good Will Hunting" fame, built on the site of the former state prison, where in 1927 Sacco and Vanzetti were executed after one of the "trials of the century."

Charred pilings to one side of the marina are remnants of Tudor Wharf, named after Frederic Tudor, Boston's ice king. Last century ice cut from local ponds, including Walden while Thoreau was in residence, was shipped as far as India. Packed in pine sawdust, two-thirds of a cargo usually survived the slow passage to Calcutta.

New England is a hard land, and has been called the only place on the planet to turn rocks and ice into export products.

Just beyond the other side of the marina is berthed the black hulled USS CONSTITUTION, which was built a few hundred yards away in the North End.

Across the harbor to the east for a few brief years Donald McKay created the greatest of the clipper ships.

To the south the white wedding cake spire of the Old North Church rises over the North End. The famed signal was not to but from Paul Revere, who after going to the church with the sexton, was rowed across the harbor to begin his ride to Lexington and legend. Needing something to muffle the oars, the girl friend of one of the men tore off a piece of her petticoat, which Paul Revere later attested salaciously was still "warm to the touch."

Closer to the waterfront the Brink's Robbery took place, and not far away is the hole left in the hearts of Boston sports fans by the demolition of the Boston Garden. Ten or twelve modern and post-modern rectangles that dominate Boston's downtown rise a few blocks inland.

Dark water connects these shores, black, brown, olive, gray, seldom blue, but no longer particularly polluted for a harbor surrounded by three million people.

Fall like spring is uncertain in Boston. Usually these seasons are brief, and some years they don't appear at all.

October is Boston's driest month and, with flaming leaves, its most beautiful. Balancing hurricane season against winter gales, a few boats head across that dark water on long planned cruises, almost invariably down the Intracoastal Waterway to Florida and the Caribbean. This year one solitary boat passed through on its way back to Canada at the end of a year away. For those of us who remain the essence of fall is the preparation for winter.

THE HAWKE OF TUONELA moves from her summer slip on G dock, which opens directly onto the harbor and so is easier to enter and exit and from which we have probably the best view in the city, to her winter quarters alongside B dock, nearer the shore. G dock is too exposed to northeasters, and moving liveaboards in simplifies maintenance and snow removal for the marina.

Fall is shrink-wrap season for most liveaboards. The sound of fall is the whoosh of propane heating torches. But not for us.

When I rebuilt THE HAWKE OF TUONELA's interior I included a thin layer of insulation. Being aboard almost constantly, I find shrink-wrapping too stuffy and confining. Most days, even in mid-winter, I open the cabin to fresh air for at least a few minutes. And our electric heating bills are less than average. Partly this is because Shatters-the-reluctant-ship's-cat and I have come to accept anything over 60ºF as satisfactory. Or at least I have. Shatters spends as much of her life as possible sitting on me, content to have forgotten that her home ever moves. One of the first things Carol does after coming home from her warmer office is turn up the heat.

As it does for people living ashore fall for us means changing screens for storm windows. Our storm windows are bubble wrap, which enables sunlight to enter. For the hatches I have backed pieces of Reflectix insulation with white headliner. In the fall, these are used only at night. One of the ways to measure the transition to winter is how regularly I find the condensation on the *inside* of the hatches frozen when I remove the Reflectix in the morning.

Fall is moving shorts and short-sleeved shirts to the back of lockers and Polartec and Levis to the front. Carol reclaims her winter coat from summer storage at the dry cleaner. Her boots somehow materialize. I try to remember where I stowed my gloves. The zipper sticks on the clothes bag the first time I want to get my leather jacket. The electric blanket and two electric heaters are pulled from their lockers and plugged in, although in fall usually only one is used. The comforter makes its way from a sail bag onto the V-berth.

One afternoon I walk over and buy some charcoal. Fortunately I remember to remove the cap that keeps water out of the chimney before lighting the fire.

The USS CONSTITUTION strikes her topmasts, one of which was broken in a northeaster a couple of years ago, a lesson apparently two hundred years in the learning.

Although the marina has been here only twenty years, the harsh climate has weathered the wooden docks so they seem older. Each fall the marina staff refurbishes the non-skid on the ramps from the main and side gates down to the docks.

I put a final coat of Deks Olje on the few pieces of teak on deck, and I finally figure out a way to finish off the sole and trim in the head.

I also change the oil in the diesel auxiliary, spray lubricant over cables and controls, and run antifreeze into the system.

Reflectix panels are velcroed into place above the half bulkhead at the ends of the quarter berths so that we don't lose heat to THE HAWKE OF TUONELA's empty stern.

The cabin lights dim and I remember to reconnect the battery charger. Days are so short, the sun so low, our solar panel is no longer enough.

One afternoon a leaf flutters through the open companionway and Shatters, who is a cat of seventeen years, becomes a kitten again, first stalking then pouncing. She bats the leaf around the cabin sole for a while before, remembering her age and dignity, she returns to curl up on my lap. I run my hand along her back and she begins to purr.

We are as ready for winter as we ever will be.

Winter

Holding the kettle under the water tap, I push down on the foot pump and encounter unexpected resistance. The pump does not spring back. For only the second time in the winters we have lived aboard in Boston the fresh water tank, located in the uninsulated stern of THE HAWKE OF TUONELA, has frozen. Levering the pedal up with my toe I manage to get a trickle of icy water. Enough finally to start coffee before crawling back over a sail stowed on a quarter berth, electric heater in hand, to thaw the tank. Carol wisely remains in bed.

Winter is frozen water. Falling from the sky. Coating hatches and decks and docks. Sheeting across the harbor. A simple process, a force of immense power, transforming the face of the planet, shattering mountains, changing lives. Frozen water especially changes the lives of those of us who live on the water, driving us inside our cabins and ourselves. We see our neighbors only briefly. A word and a nod, passing on the docks, cold too intense for lingering conversation. One of the things I like most about living on a boat is that essentially you live outside. But not during a New England winter.

It must be said that the waterfront is the most temperate spot in Boston, often 10° warmer than places only a few miles inland, and that Constitution Marina is kept relatively ice free by currents of fresh water spilling through the nearby locks at the mouth of the Charles River. During our winters in Boston ice has never been thick or lasted long, although occasionally the marina does have to use a launch as an ice breaker.

By Boston standards this winter has not been severe. There were only a few days when Carol's hair froze during the two-minute walk back to THE HAWKE OF TUONELA from her morning shower.

One of the sounds of being iced in is silence. Even in calm conditions a boat at dock moves. A breath of wind against the mast; a ripple left by a ship in the main channel, a ferry boat wake. An inch or two up and down, side to side. When motion ceases in the middle of the night, I awaken. For a moment or two I don't know why. Then I sense the stillness, hear the silence—it is like having the keel touch a soft mud bottom at anchor. A few inches away from my head, just on the other side of the hull, is ice.

Another sound of being iced in is a *sussh*, like a sled across hard pack, when wind or wake causes the hull to break free and roll against frozen harbor.

Thirty or so ducks are year-round marina residents where they have patiently trained several humans to feed them. Refusing to reward anyone who could migrate and doesn't, our contribution to their diet is minimal. Our V-berth is positioned approximately at THE HAWKE OF TUONELA's waterline. It took us a while to identify the sound of a wooden spoon clattering against the hull as ducks snacking on winter slime.

The ducks are particularly not fond of ice. Ducks swim around in small circles of open water and then in single file portage to the next patch of water. Duck feet slip on ice. Ducks fall down and look indignant. Ducks stomp ashore and impersonate rocks until conditions improve.

Snow is much less troublesome to all of us, ducks included. Boston averages 42 inches a year, but the last few years have seen more than 100 inches and as little as 15. Cities look best through filters. Even a city as beautiful as Rio de Janeiro is best from a distance, say five miles offshore or from the top of Corcovado. Distance and night hide blemishes and obliterate ugliness. So does snow. Sitting in the cabin with a glass of Laphroaig while snow flakes flutter into the cockpit is not unpleasant. Boston looks almost as attractive in the limited winter palette of gray and black and white of fresh snow as she does in the flaming colors of fall. And snow, aboard a boat, is easy to get rid of. My weapons of choice are a broom and dustpan; the former to push from the deck; the latter to scoop from the cockpit.

To all but the most hardened Bostonians winter is too long. November and December are darker, with shorter days and lower slanting sun, but for me February is the longest month of the year. Although the sun is noticeably returning, I get a kind of channel fever. I like to cross oceans. I like long passages. But a few hundred miles from the end I want to get in as traditionally do British sailors when they reach the English Channel. By February I am exceedingly bored. I want winter to be over. Even more so this year when I no longer have a cat on my lap because Shatters was not as prepared for winter as we had hoped and died two days after Christmas. She was only a small cat, but she had great presence and the cabin is emptier and colder and the winter even longer without her. I am tired of dreaming and planning. I want to do. Start projects, make improvements. Not to mention actually sail.

Every experienced sailor since Captain Cook, or probably Noah, has known that ships and sailors rot in port. By February I am rotten to the core.

Spring

I surrender to winter but I push spring. I know the precise moment it begins aboard THE HAWKE OF TUONELA

A day in March. The temperature is in the fifties. The five-day forecast is stormless. I crawl aft and open two seacocks before climbing to the cockpit where I kneel in the position of a supplicant. A moment of slight trepidation. I slip the key into the ignition. This is the instant. There have been years when the turning of that key was followed by silence. Winter corrodes wires. This year the starter motor grinds without the engine catching, until I realize that I have forgotten to engage the cold start button on the diesel, which after freezing all winter is entitled to all the help it can get. The engine coughs to life. A cloud of smoke followed by antifreeze-pink water spurts from the exhaust. Cloud and pink dissipate. The engine rumbles onward. The welcome sound of spring.

Spring is motion, spring is release from enforced dormancy, spring is being able to work on deck. For most liveaboards at Constitution Marina, spring is removing shrink-wrap and dismantling frames. Forms emerge from burrows like etiolated gophers. People living a few feet away have not been seen for months.

Spring is a review of lists and revision of priorities. Spring is visiting chandleries and phoning orders to discount houses. Spring is spending money on something worthwhile again: the boat.

The abrasions of winter must be effaced. Dock lines and fenders tied for six months inevitably mark topsides. The cockpit sole has been dinged by salt and ice. Winches need to be stripped and lubricated. Everything needs to be cleaned, and everything that is supposed to move and hasn't needs to be lubricated.

The real joys of spring are the big new projects, planned and dreamed about for months. One advantage of New England's climate is that you can usually get a discount on orders for things like masts and sails placed six months in advance. After all you certainly aren't going anywhere.

For THE HAWKE OF TUONELA this year the big projects were installing a new Monitor self-steering vane, some new sails, and our alternate year haul-out. Thoughts of converting from sloop to cutter rig remained only thoughts.

The day after I reawakened the diesel, I took the first step in preparation for the Monitor and relocated two cleats. In doing so I had to squirm into the stern, which becomes a mold colony during winter. The next day was cold. New England spring is usually fickle, promising more than it actually delivers, coming and going without warning, explanation or reason. I say usually because this year the weather soon became so good that people began to complain about it.

Two weeks did pass before a day was warm enough to open the boat for ventilation, and I crawled aft with a bucket of diluted bleach to remove life forms previously unknown to science.

For most of Constitution Marina spring begins in mid-April when the marina is reconfigured. Liveaboards huddled near the shore move out. THE HAWKE OF TUONELA returns to the far end of G dock. Water gurgles past her hull. The sense is of expansiveness and space. Our view becomes the steeple of North Church and the city skyline rather than the bow of a shrink-wrapped powerboat looming inches from our stern. The USS CONSTITUTION's cannon fired each morning at 8:00 and each evening at sunset is sensationally louder. Even the novelty of bobbing in the slip is welcome, though by summer powerboat wakes will no longer be novel or welcome.

The walk to the main building is now five times further. On laundry days I walk thirty minutes without ever leaving the marina. Five small boats occupy THE HAWKE OF TUONELA's winter space.

In two weekends the marina goes from half empty to almost full. Flowers bloom in boxes near the gates and around the office. New deck furniture is placed around the swimming pool.

New boats and new faces appear. Regulars return. There are even new dock carts. People smile.

Spring comes in small increments: the day I remove the bubble wrap insulation from the ports; the first afternoon I don't bother with a coat when I walk to the shower; the first night Carol doesn't turn on her half of the electric blanket; when I stow one of the electric heaters; and the more decisive day when I stow the second; trying to remember where I put the hatch screens—Boston does not have many mosquitoes, but even one is too many; the day I oil my bicycle and the first time I ride it.

For those of us who live here year round, spring actually sees a reduction in costs: no more winter liveaboard fee; no more metered electric bill; although for those who dock only in summer, rates are three times higher than in winter.

Days lengthen quickly.

There comes an evening when we have margaritas on deck.

Some of the resident ducks swim out from beneath the docks surrounded by clusters of baby ducklings.

And each spring for a few weeks the water is thick with jellyfish. (E-mail to Baudelaire: Are the jellyfish of winter with the snows of yesterday?)

An unexpected moment came this spring when, as I tightened the last bolt on the Monitor self-steering vane, I realized that THE HAWKE OF TUONELA is finally ready to go. There are a good many other things I plan to do and buy during the next two years, but they are refinements and could, like the cutter rig, wait five or ten thousand miles or never. After six years of owning and working on this boat as weather and finances have permitted, the Monitor was the last true essential. I could sail next week. I won't. The goal is not just to sail away, but this time to sail away for good—in all possible ways—and so I will stick to the plan. But that I could is deeply satisfying.

The best of spring is, of course, the first sail. A Saturday in late April. Uncertain blue sky. Slanting sun. Typical forecast: warmer inland; cooler along the coast. Other sailors are still working on their boats, and we have the harbor to ourselves. With water temperature still in the forties, the wind off Massachusetts Bay is cold and we keep adding fleece and foul weather gear as we make long tacks south past the city skyline, then catch a slant where the channel turns east. Under new sails—a fully battened main and a 130% furling jib—and with a freshly antifouled bottom, THE HAWKE OF TUONELA sails better than ever.

While we are tacking, Carol handles the tiller and I trim the jib, but when we settle on a long starboard leg, she gives me the helm. The boat heels. I reach forward and ease the traveler. Our speed increases to seven knots. I feel the water moving past the rudder, the wind against my skin, the sloop coming alive. How many thousands of times have I felt this? But not for seven months. We are heading east. A jog through the Narrows, then clear water off Boston Light. I engage the Monitor. It steers perfectly. With this southeast wind we could easily clear Cape Cod forty miles ahead and just keep going. With each moment, with each wave, winter recedes, becomes a distant memory, becomes impossible, now that it is spring.

Summer

A Boston matron once said, "Why should I travel when I'm already there?"

During the summer this could apply to those of us at Constitution Marina. The world comes to us. In addition to our regular neighbor, the USS CONSTITUTION, this year we also saw from our cockpit replicas of the AMERICA and of the BOUNTY, the J-boat ENDEAVOUR, and a wide variety of other craft, including the New York Yacht Club's fleet on its annual cruise.

After the resignation of fall, the endurance of winter, the hope of spring, summer at last is being: the view from the cockpit; the completion of projects; sailing.

Carol and I often have dinner on deck while lights come on downtown and evening cruise boats hover nearby, curious to see what we are eating and coincidentally observe the sunset cannon fired on the CONSTITUTION.

With a constantly open companionway, life aboard THE HAWKE OF TUONELA becomes expansive, headroom is unlimited, and the laundry bag is light.

Sounds of softball games and from children playing around the oldest public swimming pool in the country drift across the two hundred yards of water separating us from the North End. As do the muffled sounds of The Big Dig, sirens of ambulances heading to Massachusetts General, and the constant low hum of the city, to which we have become oblivious until we sail to Maine and are startled by the quiet.

Almost always we can sit and simply watch boats sail, noting who is going well and who isn't. To a sailor any boat properly trimmed is a vision of grace as paradoxically it moves without any seeming movement.

Boston is no longer a great commercial seaport, but ships pass, mostly car carriers heading to the nearby Mystic River Wharf.

The waters of our corner of the harbor are generally smooth. Two exceptions are northeasters and powerboat wakes, not from passing ships but from obnoxious fleas emerging from the Charles River locks and heading flat out for open water. New-comers to the marina yell futilely; those of us who have been here a while mutter, "Bleeping powerboats," and wait for the rocking to stop before continuing about our business.

Festivals of fireworks brighten our night skies. The display on July 4 is partially blocked by intervening structures, but is preceded a night earlier by grand pyrotechnics over the harbor and followed a few weeks later by celebrations on the CONSTITUTION's birthday. All through the summer firecrackers are set off in the predominately Italian North End on saints' days.

Summer is being able to work outside. 1999 saw our to-do list significantly reduced. Some scheduled purchases, such as replacing the autopilot that died a year ago were deferred, in this case because the Monitor steers so well; and others, such as having a small dodger made to protect the companionway were moved forward a year. As fall approached I had still to complete the installation of a new genoa track and build shelves in an attempt to bring order to the storage chaos beside the quarter berths.

And most of all summer is sailing. We shot up to Maine for a week and with only one day of fog even saw the place, and sailed on weekends to Provincetown, Gloucester, and Marblehead.

One disadvantage of Constitution Marina—the six or seven mile distance to open water—provides the compensation of being able to anchor overnight behind the harbor islands.

There is a point just south of downtown Boston where the harbor narrows, with the old fort at Castle Island to the west and Logan Airport to the east. Powerboat wakes churn the water into a cauldron while jets pass deafeningly just above the masthead. It has all the charm of a train wreck.

But less than two miles away, we enjoy more civilized Boston moments anchored between Long and Georges Islands, where after sunset THE HAWKE OF TUONELA is usually the only boat. In the city but apart from it, we sit in the evening and watch the beams of Boston Light and The Graves to the east, the arc of shore lights from south through west to north, and finish a bottle of wine while listening to a concert from Tanglewood on the radio.

Memorial Day sees a return to the marina of the summer people. Parking spaces and dock carts are more difficult to find, though less so this year than in the past; lines form to use showers and toilets; the postage stamp swimming pool is infested with children; and tourists trudge along the Freedom Trail.

1999 was a good duck year with six of seven of one brood and five of six in the other surviving to adulthood.

By June the ducklings of spring are half models; by July fractionally rigged; and by August full masthead ducks; at which time their mother seeks new amatory adventures.

Even full size young ducks are easy to distinguish. Older ducks ignore humans unless food is being offered, while young ducks, like adolescents of other species, cover inner uncertainty with a bluff of beady-eyed aggression.

Barbecues and parties are held on the deck surrounding the marina office.

Despite complaints by local Esquimaux, there are only a few truly hot days when we sit quietly under portable fans, grateful not to be suffering from chilblains.

Days shorten. And one evening we are surprised that the CONSTITUTION is firing her sunset cannon before 7:00 p.m.

For most in the marina, summer is over Labor Day. Ads for shrink-wrap ominously appear in the Sunday *Globe*. And no matter how good the September weather, the crowds do not return.

But summer must include the hurricane season, and this year Floyd came close enough to cause the marina staff to weave a web of lines between docks and shore and carry out anchors from those of us on G dock, which was last done three summers ago, while a crane lowered the CONSTITUTION's topyards. I doubled docklines and removed loose gear from deck, although I did not unbend the sails, which I would have done if I really expected serious wind. Although Floyd brought only thirty- to forty-knot gusts to Boston, not to prepare would have been imprudent.

Summer ended for me precisely at 2:00 a.m. Sunday, September 19, when I awoke cold. After a while I reluctantly rolled from bed and found the sailbag in which the comforter had been stowed since May. When I spread it over the V-berth Carol mumbled a sleepy "Thank you."

I crawled back into bed and fall.

December 11, 2000

In the early evening of December 11, 2000, six months before our five-year plan was complete, I sat in THE HAWKE OF TUONELA's cabin and thought: twenty-five years ago tonight there was a rising gale off Cape Horn. I knew because I was there. Fifty-four days out of San Diego alone aboard EGREGIOUS, from whose cracked hull I was bailing seven tons of water every twenty-four hours.

At the same time, five or six thousand miles north in Florida, THE HAWKE OF TUONELA was being built.

And a few hundred miles still further north in Charlotte, North Carolina, Carol was attending classes as a senior in high school.

For several days preceding December 11, 1975, the sky had been overcast, so I could not get sextant sights. Although this was the start of the southern summer, each day had seen some sleet and snow. I never slept long, but when I could see my hands in the first weak light of dawn, my fingers were swollen like sausages from exposure to the near freezing water I dragged from the bilge.

Finally on December 11 the sun became faintly visible through clouds for two brief intervals, and I drew positions lines I believed in enough to make a running fix and turn east.

I remembered the joy when late in the afternoon, while sitting in the companionway eating spaghetti from a pot, I saw a vague silhouette of land before me, the rocky islets of the Diego Ramirez group, thirty or forty miles southeast of Horn Island. It was perhaps *the* moment of my life. I knew that no matter what happened, even if the mast fell down, on the next day I would be blown east and become the first American to round Cape Horn alone.

During the night the gale increased to full Force Twelve.

By dawn of December 12, the Aries windvane could not steer, so for one of the few times in my voyages, I tied myself in the cockpit and steered all day, making seven and eight knots under bare poles.

I had read Chichester's book—it was his record for the fastest solo circumnavigation in a monohull that I was in the process of breaking—but was skeptical of his description of waves cresting abruptly when he crossed onto the continental shelf. Sometimes you have to see for yourself, and I did. In the space of a few miles the waves began to break just as Sir Francis said they would. For me they even broke in two directions: from the southwest ahead of the wind, and from the northwest as they re-bounded off invisible land.

I saw nothing but water and a few albatross that obviously belonged in the Southern Ocean more than I did. Sensing the rhythm of the waves, I was able to steer through the maelstrom safely, except for one wave that caught me by surprise and skewed us sideways. I had to brace myself with my feet across the cockpit and use both hands and all my strength on the tiller to bring EGREGIOUS back under control. Twenty-five years later I could still feel the solid resistance against the tiller.

Around nightfall the wind fell from Force Twelve back to a mere gale and I was able to re-engage the Aries, from whose servo rudder a rooster tail had often risen as we surfed down waves, and go below for a celebratory dinner of canned stew.

I was cold, tired, battered, frostbitten, and perfectly happy. Water sloshing over the floorboards had come from the Pacific Ocean and, after I ate, would be thrown into the Atlantic. Cape Horn was behind me.

Cape Horn will always be one of the ends of the earth, but in 1975 it was a barely explored frontier. In addition to being the first American, I was only the eighth or ninth man to round the Horn alone, and, as far as I know, the first to do so in a modern fin keel/spade rudder boat. I was sailing from the age of bi-planes.

On December 11, 2000, the wind was light off Cape Horn, less than ten knots. I knew because I had looked at the satellite weather map on the Web site of the Vendée Globe yacht race.

When in a few minutes Carol came home from work we would celebrate with a glass or two of Laphroaig single malt scotch.

Boston Harbor and Cape Horn. Both cold in December. Separated by twenty-five years of time and chance.

Ernest Hemingway always had Paris. I have Cape Horn.

PART II

RETURN TO THE SEA

8 *Return to the Sea*

Good-bye

Good-bye. We said good-bye and good-bye and then we said good-bye again.

We said good-bye in offices and we said good-bye on docks. As student and architect Carol had been in Harvard Square for almost twenty years. We had lived aboard in Constitution Marina for five years. One of Carol's friends attended five different good-bye parties for her.

Friday, May 18, was Carol's last day in the office. On my birthday several years earlier, she had given me a jar full of beans with a card saying, "Throw a bean overboard every day and your dream will come true." We jointly threw the last bean into Boston Harbor that morning. Fortunately the water under our slip was 40 feet deep so we expected to be far away when the beanstalks finally broke the surface.

We were given hats, T-shirts, bottles of wine, Champagne, and a bottle of Laphroaig older than I usually drink. Before my first circumnavigation I observed that departing is an alcoholic's dream. Everyone wants to buy you a drink.

Carol was given a Luminox watch, identical to my passage watch, and a digital camera, and a countdown clock showing the remaining time until her final big project, a medical research building for the University of Massachusetts, would be completed.

We sold one bicycle and gave away the other. We gave away our American television and bought a multi-system model that can be used in most of the world.

Carol cleared the boat of some oversized architecture books and the last of her work wardrobe and suddenly we had two empty lockers into which I built shelves for food storage.

On Thursday of Carol's first week among the unemployed, we said good-bye to Route 1, Boston's contribution to the world of strip malls, and the home of two chandleries, a propane filling station, and a supermarket. Driving home we said good-bye to the Tobin Bridge.

On Friday we went sailing for the first time since the preceding fall. I had raised, lowered, lubricated, painted, gone up the mast to check the rig, and done all the other routine things, and was confident that the boat was ready, but still it was nice actually to sail.

We gave away Carol's loyal and still reliable, but aged and rusty Honda Prelude. While we were out on the harbor, an adoption charity came and towed it away. When we returned the parking space was empty. So we turned in our parking cards to the marina.

Now foot bound, which in Boston is not inconvenient, we limited ourselves to shopping at the local Foodmaster and a stroll downtown for film and books.

On our last night we had dinner at the nearby restaurant where we had eaten just after we first met seven years earlier.

As we returned to the marina we said good-bye to the Bunker Hill Monument.

But it did not seem real. It felt no different than just another summer cruise to Maine or Martha's Vineyard. It did not feel as though this time we were really leaving. We had thought and longed for it for so many years, only the longing was real.

Disconnect

The Internet really does change everything. It even creates new hazards of the sea.

I routinely awaken between 5:00 and 6:00 a.m. The marina office opens at 9:00. So I told the staff that we would almost certainly be gone by then and would, after taking a final shower, drop our keys in the slot.

THE HAWKE OF TUONELA was attached to the dock by four lines: two bow lines, a starboard stern line and spring line; and by three cables: television, telephone, and power.

I had already arranged to have the telephone and television disconnected the following day, but had kept my Earthlink account open so I could make a final weather check on the Internet, particularly the Bermuda weather site, which I had found provides the most convenient access to maps of the North Atlantic from Boston to the Azores. I had already ascertained that the Earthlink service would be stopped immediately upon my making a telephone call to them.

I had expected to be too excited to sleep, but then our departure did not seem real and I slept well, woke at 5:00, got up, made some coffee, turned on the computer, went online, checked the Bermuda maps. Everything still looked okay. The wind should be behind us for a couple of days and nothing terrible was looming to the west, and that is the most you can hope for from the North Atlantic.

I disconnected—or so I thought—shut down the computer and awakened Carol. I should have let her sleep. Earthlink's customer service was a recorded message: "Our office is closed from midnight to 5:00 a.m. Pacific Time."

At a few minutes after 8:00 a.m. Eastern Time a polite man answered the phone. He asked why I wanted to terminate service and when I told him said that they offer satellite service. "Not in my price range yet," I replied.

By the time we had showered, there were people in the marina office. When I handed them our keys, one of them said, "I thought you were already gone."

I did not explain.

I removed the telephone and television cords from the boat and left them on the dock for the marina to have as spares. I removed the power cord from the dock and kept it on the boat, as we did charts of the Eastern seaboard, just in case something critical broke within the first few hundred miles and we had to come back.

We started the new Yanmar, which had replaced the aging Volvo a year earlier; and with Carol at the tiller, I tossed the port bow line aboard. The spring and stern lines were next. Only the starboard bow line was left. Carol put the diesel in reverse and slowly began to back into glassy Boston Harbor. I walked the bow back until, when the shrouds were even with the end of the side tie, I stepped aboard. Nothing held us to the country in which I had been born almost sixty years earlier. I did not know that I would ever see it again.

Disconnect.

The Captain

A light west wind blew over and around the Boston skyline.

I raised the main and, in bright sunshine, we motorsailed across a harbor crossed only by a ferryboat.

We looked back and said good-bye to Boston, good-bye to the cranes of the Big Dig, and, with a nod to East Boston to port, good-bye to Captain Slocum, although we would see him many times again: in the Azores, Gibraltar, Rio de Janeiro, Cape Town, Sydney.

I reread *Sailing Alone Around the World* for the third or fourth time while living aboard in Boston. Each time I brought something more to the book: as a teenager in the Midwest only hope; as a man in my late thirties while sailing an 18′ open boat during my second circumnavigation, some experience of the sea and of attempting what others thought to be impossible; and this last time considerable more experience of the sea and Boston winters, of which THE HAWKE OF TUONELA endured six and the SPRAY one.

The Slocum Society discovered a newspaper clipping stating that SPRAY spent her winter tied to the National Docks in East Boston, while the captain stayed ashore. On April 24, 1895, the wind being fair he set sail—for Gloucester.

I had the sense in reading his book, this last time, that the good captain was feeling his way. He must have had some doubts about what he was undertaking. Of course he was early in the season for the North Atlantic and had time in hand. From Gloucester he sailed to a harbor in Maine, which the cruising guides warn you is now packed with private moorings, and then to Nova Scotia where he was born.

We had been to Gloucester, so the wind being fair on the morning of May 29, 2001, we sailed directly for the Azores. To which we had also been, but prefer.

The Rubber Band

It is seven miles winding through harbor islands from Constitution Marina to Boston Light.

When we reached open water off the light, with nothing but the northern tip of Cape Cod to clear some forty miles ahead, we turned off the diesel and set the jib. While we ate lunch the Monitor steered and THE HAWKE OF TUONELA slid east at three knots. We carry 18 gallons of fuel and were not going to power 2000 miles.

For years as we summer sailed I had told Carol that I was living for the day when the Boston skyline disappeared for good below the western horizon.

But we had been on a rubber band and when we sailed to Gloucester or Provincetown or up to Maine or down to Martha's Vineyard, it always snapped us back.

Now as we looked astern, the Boston skyline remained obstinately in place, and nothing seemed any different. It still did not feel as though we were really leaving.

Not until late afternoon did I turn and find the western horizon empty; but by then the eastern horizon held land and, with the coming of night, the lights of Provincetown.

The rubber band did not stretch until it broke as much as, toward the end of the first week, it simply disappeared.

Passing just north of George's Bank, we dodged fishing boats for two nights, and we crossed the shipping route between Europe and New York. The ocean seemed crowded not open.

Only after the fourth day did we have the world to ourselves, and I looked around at the waves as THE HAWKE OF TUONELA danced east and thought: all those years I was in Boston, *this* was always here.

I went below and gathered the East Coast charts, carried them on deck and threw them overboard. Even if something broke we were not going back. And the voyage became real.

The Barometer

I said to a friend who has crossed the North Atlantic many times, "I am really looking forward to settling into the rhythms of an ocean passage again." And he replied thoughtfully, "I don't know that I have ever done that." It was only much later that I remembered that he has only sailed in the North Atlantic.

A magazine reporter said to me, "You have written that the North Atlantic is your least favorite ocean." I said, "Yes. And it still is." "But you are going to sail it again." We were in Boston. I waved my hand vaguely to the east and replied, "It is the only ocean out there."

The essential image of the passage is THE HAWKE OF TUONELA heeled 10° to 15° on a starboard close reach, powering smoothly through waves at seven to eight knots. I have the starboard berth in the main cabin; Carol the port; so I am always climbing over my lee cloth. Or I am sitting on deck simply reveling as the sloop sails. There is such pleasure in that: in feeling her move, perfectly balanced, the Monitor steering, everything in tune, not powering her way through the water as much as slicing as cleanly as a sharp knife.

Yet it was not a fast passage: 17 days for 2,000 nautical miles. We kept coming back to that image, but we did not sustain it.

We carry two barometers aboard. Both are digital. Both move together, although sometimes they are a millibar apart. They moved a lot. In 17 days we had four highs, three lows, one of them a gale, and were flat becalmed twice.

One night we went to bare poles in the gale, though not of absolute necessity. Under the equivalent of triple reefed main and deeply furled jib, the sloop was sailing well, but getting beaten up by the waves more than I liked, so we eased off for a few hours.

The next night we went to bare poles in a flat calm to prevent unnecessary chaff of the sails and stress on the rig as we flopped around.

The third morning out the temperature dropped into the low forties and, shivering, we dug out long underwear, gloves and watch caps.

Later that day we reached the Gulf Stream and the ocean temperature leaped from 49° to 71° and we changed into shorts.

That is the North Atlantic. That is why it is my least favorite ocean and why my friend has never been able to settle into the rhythms of an ocean passage.

Repairs

Although at various times the rudder shrieked incessantly and we lost the autopilot, the primary bilge pump, the jib furling gear, and the entire electrical system, it was an uneventful passage.

One of the biggest mistakes people who are preparing to go sailing make is not sailing their boats. The second biggest mistake is not getting their bodies in shape.

We were partially guilty of the first.

I had sailed THE HAWKE OF TUONELA almost 10,000 miles prior to our departure, but only a few of those miles since major changes had been made the preceding summer, including a planned replacement of the rudder and rudder bearings and an unplanned replacement of the diesel engine. The engine cost us the summer, not to mention $10,000, and by the time the work was done winter was upon us.

The noise from the rudder began less than fifty miles out. It had in fact begun on our sail the Friday before we left, but was then cured by a spray of McLube, which at sea proved inadequate.

Fortunately the sound was not from a misaligned bearing as I first feared, but friction where the tiller is supported at the deck. A previous owner had screwed a block of wood to the underside of the tiller to keep it elevated to a convenient height. Being taller I had added a second block of wood to increase the elevation. These rode smoothly on a sheet of Teflon screwed to the deck, which had to be removed when the new rudder was installed. The blocks of wood now rubbed against an aluminum collar.

The solution was obviously to elevate the tiller so those two points did not meet. Poised precariously between tiller lines from the Monitor, I duct taped a scrap of teak to the rudder shaft cap fitting, creating a gap, which brought the tiller's and our misery to a silent end.

The morning after the gale, the wind was still at twenty-five knots and we were being rolled around by eight-foot waves. Carol, who was sitting at the chart table, said, "The chartplotter is not working."

I flipped a couple of switches and found that nothing was working because we had no battery power.

THE HAWKE OF TUONELA's two batteries were under Carol, who easily moved, and the valise-packed life raft, which was less easily moved. One of the main cables had broken at the terminal connection. This was a ground cable to the engine and I expect that when the new Yanmar was installed the old cable was used. It seemed to be long enough at the dock, but was just a tad too short for the inevitable movement at sea.

Although I do not carry an enormous number of spares, I did have an extra terminal fitting, which I pressed on the wire and reattached. I also cut another scrap of wood and screwed it as a spacer into the battery compartment.

With power restored, we found that everything worked

except the bilge pump. I don't know that there is a causal relationship, but after checking for loose wires, I found that it needed a new fuse, which I duly replaced.

While the Monitor does almost all the steering, we were powering through a flat mid-afternoon calm two hundred miles west of the Azores with the autopilot in charge. Both of us were down below when I noticed the sun racing across the sky.

The autopilot connects to a bracket on the underside of the tiller held by two bolts, one of which had sheered off. As the autopilot frantically tried to get us back on compass course, the broken bolt carved chunks from the tiller.

When I buy bolts or screws I usually buy a few extra, which I throw into large kitchen canisters. I found the spare bolt and put the autopilot back to work.

So some potentially serious problems were easily solved by a few scraps of wood, duct tape, and two pieces of metal costing a dollar or two. The joker was that they pretty much had to be those exact pieces of metal.

I have sailed boats without engines and without electrical systems around the world, and have confidence that I can sail THE HAWKE OF TUONELA anywhere and anchor. But having paid for the things, I would like for them to work.

The jib furling gear caused the most grief and was entirely my own fault.

THE HAWKE OF TUONELA is a three-sail boat: fully battened main, 130% furling jib, and cruising spinnaker. So was my last boat, RESURGAM, in which I made a couple of circumnavigations using only those three sails. More sails are aboard, as they were on RESURGAM, but I have not set anything other than the basic three in more than twenty years.

THE HAWKE OF TUONELA's furling gear is Profurl, which has a metal tang extending from the upper swivel to a slot in a plastic collar on the headstay to prevent the halyard from wrapping.

When I set the spinnaker to starboard, it is raised on the winch normally used by the jib halyard.

Late on the afternoon that the tiller pilot fitting broke, a light wind blew from the north and I set the spinnaker to starboard, easing off the jib halyard when I removed it from the winch. You can see this coming. When a couple of hours later I lowered the spinnaker sock and tried to set the jib, I forgot to take up the slack in the halyard. The jib unfurled about halfway and stopped. I tugged on the sheet, then refurled the jib and tried again with the same result. I furled the jib and stared up at the masthead and called myself unflattering names.

We could sail the last two hundred miles under main and half jib, or the flanker if the wind permitted, or set the working jib flying, or I could go up the mast.

We have several ways to go up the mast: a mainsail track webbing ladder, a variation on a mountain climbing bosun chair by ATN, or just being winched. In port I usually go up the webbing ladder wearing a bosun chair attached to the spare main halyard which Carol tails for me.

The seas were nearly flat, but marked by a few swells. The fastest and safest way now was to be winched. And Carol was clamoring for the exercise. Well, perhaps not.

I have been to the masthead at sea only once before and that on a boat with a mast shorter than THE HAWKE OF TUONELA's 50 feet above deck. Up close and personal the laws of physics are quite impressive. At the end of a long lever you get thrown around a lot. The view is probably spectacular. I did not enjoy it. And it took three weeks for the bruises on my thighs and arms to fade.

The wrap at the masthead was easily unsnarled.

I subsequently kept more tension on the jib halyard than was probably necessary.

The Breath

Many of us live with tension so constant that it becomes transparent until a change in intensity brings it back to mind.

Decades ago in San Diego when I had what is called a real

job, I found that sometimes when I went daysailing out beyond Point Loma and got into the open ocean, I would unconsciously take a deep breath and suddenly become aware that the constant tension had vanished.

On the afternoon of Thursday, June 7, at approximately 40°N, 48°W, while sitting on deck as THE HAWKE OF TUONELA closereached east at the customary seven knots, I took such a breath. It had been years. So long that I had forgotten. The breath cannot be willed; it simply comes. But it felt so good I took another.

Channel Fever

Channel fever is dependent upon expectation. I have frequently spent several months at sea, but on passages that at departure I expected to take months: New Zealand around the Horn to Uruguay in a 36-foot sloop; Singapore to Aden in an 18-foot open boat; and San Diego around the Horn east to New Zealand in a 37-foot cutter.

Boston to Horta is two thousand nautical miles. The expectation was sixteen days, plus or minus two.

So when we were becalmed two hundred miles west of Horta on the fifteenth day, we powered through the afternoon. We had wanted nothing more than to be at sea, but our mind set was sixteen days and now we wanted to be in. I wanted a shower and Carol, whose neck hurt, just wanted to be stopped, motionless and still.

The move was tactical. Certainly I would have powered through a calm the last few miles to reach the harbor before dark, so why not power now rather than sit and roll around. The hope was that the wind would return, which after four hours it did, with the unexpected bonus of a trip up the mast.

Despite such extravagant use of the engine, we reached Horta with half of a fuel tank left, making our consumption about two gallons per 1000 miles. At this rate we would definitely have to find a fuel dock within a year.

Someplace Else

Sometimes it all comes together and is perfect.

I wanted to be in by Friday sunset. We arrived at Friday dawn and deliberately slowed down for that.

While becalmed I had told Carol that we wanted wind from the north or south at 15 knots. We got north at 15 knots, and the teal sloop beam reached due east at speed under a blue sky flecked by a few white clouds, until I finally had to partially furl the jib to delay our arrival.

Just at sunset we saw the first sail of the passage, coming up from the south, presumably from Bermuda.

Carol caught the first sight of land, lights on the west end of Faial before midnight, and the first sweet earthy smell of land during her watch near dawn.

When I came on deck at 5:00 a.m. we were nine miles due south of Horta, the wind largely blocked by the island. I turned on the diesel and furled the sails.

It was a clear and beautiful morning. The green terraced fields on the slopes of Faial to our west; the high cone of Pico silhouetted to the east against the rising sun.

As we powered north two other sails became visible behind us.

From the sea, the red tiled rooftops of Horta looked little changed, but just after 7:00 we rounded the breakwater and I gave a surprised, "Oh, no!"

Boats were anchored and rafted everywhere. The reception dock was buried behind two rows six boats deep with a catamaran on the side for good measure. The quiet peaceful harbor of my memory is no more.

Still we had arrived and were where I had wanted to be for years: someplace else.

9 The Azores

We spent a month in the Azores: two weeks in Horta; a week and a half at two harbors on Terceira; and several days at Ponta Delgada on São Miguel.

The Azores are green hills, whitewashed walls, red tile roofs, stone fenced fields, churches, monasteries, and fortifications. Although there is still a feeling of remoteness from the U.S. and mainland Europe, with Portuguese membership in the EEC, change has come to the islands. For sailors, one change is a number of new marinas, and another is overcrowding. Like some American national parks, parts of the Azores are being loved to death.

When we arrived in Horta after the passage from Boston I was surprised to find the harbor so crowded. Crowded is inadequate. Filled to overflowing. Bursting at the seams. I soon learned that not one but two rallies were in port: the return ARC from the Caribbean to Europe and an Ocean Cruising Club rally from the United Kingdom.

I suppose I understand why some people want to take part in rallies for reasons of insecurity and/or sociability and why some harbors solicit their business. An Azorean tourist newspaper proudly trumpeted that six rallies were scheduled to visit the islands that summer. This may be good for business—but then Carol and I spend money ashore too and, not having a schedule to keep, generally stay longer than rally people. It may be good for the ralliers. But it unquestionably alters the landscape, or rather seascape, and is not good for the rest of us who don't want to cross oceans in herds.

Horta Marina in June 2001 was jammed beyond tolerance or

Rafted in overcrowded Horta Marina. Horta, Faial, The Azores

safety. So many boats were rafted together on the reception dock that the wake from a local fishing boat snapped a cleat on the innermost vessel and an entire row veered out of control. Boats were five and six deep against the wall, leaving dangerously little space for maneuvering. A storm would have wrought havoc.

Carol and I were in fact mostly fortunate in our immediate neighbors: a quiet French couple inside and, most of the time, a British couple on the outside. An Irish sailor on a nearby boat did his best to maintain stereotypes by falling drunk into the harbor one midnight while trying to climb from boat to boat. Still there is minimal privacy; people walk across your deck at all hours; and a party on a neighboring boat, even a quiet one, is effectively taking place in your cockpit. In addition to having to move whenever a boat inside you does. We in fact left Horta a day earlier than planned because the French couple informed us Sunday afternoon that they intended to depart Monday morning about 8:00.

This turned out better for us than the French. Rather than un-raft and reraft and do the whole thing again on Tuesday, we got free at 7:45 Monday and went up to the five-deep reception dock, cleared for Angra do Heroismo on Terceira Island, and had a splendid sail, covering 70 miles and unexpectedly reaching the harbor before sunset. The following day, when we had originally intended to leave, it rained.

It took about an hour for us to clear from Horta and we wondered why the French boat, a big Amel, did not appear before we sailed.

A few days later in Angra we learned that a line from the British boat had caught on the Amel's bow thruster. The Frenchman had to dive to cut and untangle the line and finally got away at noon. Another intimate joy of rafting.

One day when for a few hours no one was rafted outside of us, we decided we would be happier at anchor and got permission to move, but before we could do so another boat shifted alongside us and so we remained in place.

Marina expansion was underway, which when complete would nearly double the number of slips, but the number of boats visiting Horta is increasing too rapidly for new construction to keep pace. The official number of visiting boats for the year 2000 was 1,144, and I estimate that there must have been at least 200 in the harbor when we were there in June 2001.

Ashore Horta remains quaint and pleasant, with narrow cobblestone streets, whose even narrower sidewalks are inlayed with mosaics. In the town museum, which I had never previously visited, a full range of the mosaics is displayed, along with a stunning collection of fig wood carvings, mostly of ships, by Faial's Euclides Silveira da Rosa. They alone are worth putting up with the crowding in the marina.

Stunning also was the view from the restaurant Vista da Baia in the tiny village of Varadouro on the south coast, where, on a day we rented a car and drove around the island, we had barbecued chicken (frango in Portuguese) for lunch after wandering about the moonscape of volcanic destruction at the old lighthouse at Ponta dos Capelinhos caused by the 1957-58 eruption.

Angra do Heroismo, to which we sailed from Horta, near the center of the south coast of Terceira is the best natural harbor in the Azores, although wide open to the southeast. The town is picturesque, historic and hilly. A hike to the biggest supermarket requires Sherpas and oxygen. If an ocean passage causes sailors to lose leg muscles, the Azores quickly rebuilds them.

The mole built to protect the marina from the exposed southeast has dramatically changed the appearance of the harbor. In July 2001 the marina was in operation, though still under construction. Almost all prices in the Azores in 2001 were incredibly low for those converting from US dollars. THE HAWKE OF TUONELA at 37 feet overall falls into the European 10-12 meter range, in Horta we paid $7 a day, and prior to the official opening of the Angra marina a slip for a boat our size cost only $4 a day.

Despite an odd surge that ricochets around inside the breakwater and is hard on dock lines, we spent several enjoyable days at Angra, which happened to coincide with a local festival. An amusement park of portable rides was set up near the marina, including a slide in the form of the upraised stern of the sinking TITANIC, down which children screamingly reenacted scenes from the movie.

On Sunday the rocky road running along the shore between the marina and the commercial part of the harbor was the scene of a local tradition of bull baiting.

We joined the crowd and watched as bulls were let out of pens. A long rope was attached to them and eight or ten young men were attached to the rope as a kind of sea anchor. They didn't keep the bull from moving, but they did more or less keep him under control, while other young men ran around and made brave gestures.

No one is much harmed by this. The bull is not pricked or stabbed or killed, and occasionally he catches one of the young men and with a satisfied grunt tosses him about. None of the young men appeared to be injured, although one did lose his pants.

One day when we didn't have to trek to the supermarket, we used our new muscles to hike up past the fortifications on

Carol at the ruins of the old lighthouse at Ponta dos Capelinhos, Faial Island, The Azores

Mount Brazil, which forms the west side of the harbor. The views over the island are spectacular. We lingered there, imagining Vasco da Gama stumbling in after his epic voyage to India—his brother died and is buried at Angra; treasure fleets dropping anchor on their way from the Americas to Iberia; Sir Francis Drake darting around the headland on a raid to try to steal that gold; and thousands of other ships and sailors over the past five centuries.

A few miles away on the east side of the island the bay at Praia da Victoria, naturally wide open to the east, has by the construction of two long breakwaters now become the biggest and best all weather anchorage in the Azores. It also was the quietest, most convenient and most pleasant spot we visited.

A marina was also under construction at Praia, but it seems unnecessary except as a dinghy landing. The anchorage is perfect and so big—the enclosed bay is over a mile long and a half-

mile wide—that if swell makes a spot uncomfortable, one simply moves to a more protected corner of the bay.

We stayed longer at Praia than we had planned, sharing this
expanse with a changing population of only four or five other
boats at a time.

One dawn we were awakened by an anchor chain rattling
out seemingly just off our bow. Although I assumed this was a
distortion of sound carrying in stillness, I got up and found a
German boat less than a boat length away. Five people were on
deck anxiously measuring the decreasing distance between our
hulls. They could have done so with a ruler. I glanced about to
see if hundreds of boats had filled the bay overnight. They had
not. Only four other boats in a mile of water. I declared conver-
sationally,—they were so close there was no need to shout—
"You are not going to stay there." And one of them said, "No."
And they moved a few hundred yards away.

About 90 miles southeast of Praia, on the largest island in the
group, São Miguel, is the largest city in the Azores, Ponta Delgada, with a long established marina and a busy, but somewhat
dirty commercial harbor.

São Miguel deserved more of our attention; but by the time
we reached Ponta Delgada, we had spent a month in the islands
and, while we had limitless time—or so I thought—we were still
subject to the seasons and needed to move on. We ignored the
attractions of São Miguel, including lakes and geysers, ate a bad
pizza and saw a bad movie (in Portugal as in Brazil American
movies are shown in English with Portuguese subtitles) and
sailed for Lisbon.

10 *Portuguese Moments*

Sailors coming from the west tend to feel when they reach the Azores that they have crossed the ocean; but a thousand miles of often rough water still separates them from continental Europe, with frequent gales moving out of the Bay of Biscay, winds blowing from the north so regularly that they are known as the Portuguese Trades, and the busiest shipping lanes in the world.

Except for the shipping, which we had to dodge our last night at sea, including one huge brightly lit object that confused me until we got close enough to see that it was a section of bridge under tow, and a Portuguese patrol boat that blasted out of the darkness at thirty knots, blinded us with searchlights as it ran alongside, failed to respond to my attempt to talk to it on the VHF, and finally roared off to disturb someone else, we made the crossing in an uneventful seven days and the eighth dawn found us off the wide mouth of the Tagus River.

Two old forts guard the river mouth and the wealth that flowed to it from India, China, Japan, Africa, and Brazil: one on the mainland to the north; the other surrounded by water on shallows to the south. Having slowed to delay our arrival, we entered the Tagus not long after first light. A ship passed in gray mist heading out, as ships have headed out for hundreds of years.

A sailor cannot help but be in awe of the place.

In the space of a single generation following Vasco Da Gama's voyage in 1497-99 this tiny nation, with a population then of only one million, brought the West and the East together, invented the idea of empire based on sea power, and made the world round. Although Americans know much more about

Columbus because he "discovered" us, da Gama's was much the more difficult, and perhaps, more momentous, voyage. Certainly it was seen as such at the time, when it almost immediately made Portugal, through control of the spice routes, the richest nation in Europe for a brief time, which I think of as The Portuguese Moment.

A strong outgoing four-knot tide slowed our progress up the Tagus. It took THE HAWKE OF TUONELA all morning to inch her way seven miles to the Doca de Alcantara marina inside a converted basin just beyond a sister bridge to San Francisco's Golden Gate. Although the outside of the dock is still a working facility for cruise and container ships, the inside is protected and reasonably quiet, despite ambulance sirens, bridge traffic, and midnight music from a nightclub ashore named Queens.

We lingered in Lisbon for several reasons, among them that the daily rate for THE HAWKE OF TUONELA in the marina was $15, but paying by the month reduced that to $7, so that a month improbably cost less than two weeks.

In addition to economy of scale, August is *the* vacation month for Europeans, and facilities, including marinas, are packed. I prefer to find a satisfactory spot and remain there until the continent calms down. And we wanted time to savor Lisbon's faded charm.

As a sailor I admired the Portuguese long before I first sailed to Portugal in 1983.

In sailing the world I have been most impressed by three achievements: the single generation in which tiny Portugal exploded over the globe and justifiably claimed to be "first in all oceans"; the earlier expansion of Islam in a few centuries from the Arabian Peninsula to islands just off Australia in one direction and the west coast of Africa in the other; and the British Empire. All were creations of people with relatively small populations who took incredible risks because they believed in themselves and their own myths. It did not matter that the myths were not real, only that they were believed in. As a child I made up my own myth about myself and then I lived it. Myths may be all we have.

I also admire Portuguese writers, particularly the poets, Luis Vaz de Camões and Fernando Pessoa, and the novelist, José Saramago, and wanted to look for traces of them in Lisbon.

Camões was born just after the generation of great voyages and wrote the Portuguese national epic, *The Lusiads*, largely about Vasco da Gama.

Pessoa lived in the first decades of last century and is considered to be, along with Cavafy, Kafka, Borges, and T.S. Eliot, one of the major figures of modernism.

José Saramago is still alive, having won the Nobel Prize for Literature in 1998. Of his novels my favorites are *Baltasar and Blimunda* and *The Year of the Death of Ricardo Reis*. After years of living in Rio de Janeiro Ricardo Reis returns to Lisbon aboard a ship which makes its way up the Tagus and docks at Alcantara. As I reread the novel in Lisbon I could look up from THE HAWKE OF TUONELA's cockpit and see him stepping ashore in 1932.

The city, which sprawls for miles over the hills on the north side of the Tagus, was destroyed by an earthquake on All Saints' Day in 1755, and in the summer of 2001 was still being rebuilt. Or so it seemed. Many of the major squares were filled with dust and heavy construction equipment, and even the 92-foot high statue of Christ on the south bank of the river was covered with scaffolding. The tourist season seems an odd time to tear up a city, but the work in Lisbon has been going on for so long that it cannot reasonably be stopped for summer tourists.

Reconstruction of the city under the direction of the Marquês de Pombal began in fact almost immediately after the earthquake, which was one of the seminal events of European history, coming as it did in an age of increasing religious skepticism. The deaths of thousands, many crushed in collapsing churches, caused intellectual debate across the continent, and resulted in, among other works of literature, Voltaire's novel, *Candide*, in which Doctor Pangloss doggedly proclaims that this is the best of all possible worlds despite some evidence to the contrary.

Having come this time to Lisbon to look for writers as well as seafarers, we quickly found that Pessoa, who in the best poetic tradition was almost unknown and unpublished in his lifetime, has one hundred years after his birth become a growth industry. The first sign of this is a statue of the man, with a head as a book, under the arch leading from the Praça do Comercio to Rua Augusta, one of the city's most prominent locations.

Later we found another statue of Pessoa sitting at a table outside one of his former haunts, the Café Brasileira in the Chiado district, and another in the cloisters of the Jeronimos Monastery. Copies of his books are for sale everywhere.

Camões, also little known and appreciated during his lifetime, has had a four hundred year head start gaining laurels and looks down at Pessoa at the Café Brasileira from his own square a short block away. Camões' tomb is opposite Vasco da Gama's at the entrance to the church at the Jeronimos Monastery, while Pessoa remains buried with his mother in a conventional cemetery.

Only Saramago, who resides in the city, cannot be found on public display, and he knows—I expect with some bemusement—that his place in the national pantheon awaits.

Rua Augusta is now a wide pedestrian mall, with shops, sidewalk cafes, street performers, and hustlers—we were offered semi-surreptitiously a camera, watches, sunglasses, and gold chains. A few blocks inland, to the right of the scaffolding covering the national theater (which hopefully will not be in place forever) is Rua das Portas de Santa Antao, a narrow street where I have had memorable shrimp. I used to say they were the best in the world, but I found their equal earlier that summer in the Azores. Long before mad cow disease Portugal was a country for seafood.

One day we visited the Museu Calouste Gulbenkian. Mr. Gulbenkian was an Armenian who helped put together oil companies and owned 5% of several, including Shell and British Petroleum, which provided him with his lucrative nickname, "Mister Five Percent." During World War II he emigrated to neutral Portugal and upon his death in 1955 left $225 million dollars and his art collection to the country.

In 1955 $225 million was real money, and it built an attractive museum that houses Mr. Gulbenkian's collection, spanning 4,000 years and including Rembrandt's, oriental vases, Egyptian cats, and some splendidly gaudy serpentine Lalique jewelry.

We ate lunch that day at a restaurant overlooking the Parque Eduardo VII, a wide green swath stretching down toward an equestrian statue of the Marquês de Pombal and the city center, before boarding a bus and riding out to Belém, about four miles west.

Coming up the Tagus on our arrival we had passed the Tower of Belém, which was originally built as a fort out in the river, but after centuries of landfill is now nearly on the shore, and the adjacent Monument to the Discoveries, whose appropriate prow-like shape juts out over the water. The view from the top of the monument, reached by elevator and stairs, is vertiginous and spectacular.

Just across the street is the Monastery, yet something must be said about that street. Automobiles are an abomination in all old cities—perhaps all cities period—but in few more than Lisbon, which has built a wide thoroughfare near the river that must be crossed over by elevated walkways or crossed under by dank tunnels and is an unmitigated city planning disaster.

Having survived that transit, one cannot miss the Monastery, where Vasco da Gama spent his last night before setting out for India and now spends all eternity. The monastery church also houses the tombs of many kings, including an empty one for King Sebastian.

The myth of Sebastianism is a unique Portuguese madness. Having been called mad myself a time or two I say that with due respect. Of Sebastian, Pessoa wrote:

> What's a man who isn't mad
> But some ruddy beast,
> A corpse postponed that breeds?

If The Portuguese Moment began with Vasco da Gama, it clearly ended with King Sebastian, 1557-1578, who in blind religious fervor and complete military incompetence led an army of 20,000, including the entire Portuguese nobility, against the Moors. In the space of four hours one day in June at Alacer-Kebir in present day Morocco, the Portuguese were annihilated.

More than 8,000 were killed, including the boy-king, and the rest were captured and sold into slavery. Fewer than one hundred escaped to the coast and safety.

So complete and unbelievable was the defeat that the Portuguese went into denial and have never come out. A myth developed that Sebastian and the army had not died but lived on in the Isles of the Blessed and would one day return to save Portugal in an hour of need.

Thus the empty tomb awaiting The Desired One.

Of the battle, Camões, who had returned to Portugal after spending most of his adult life in India and Macao, wrote, "I so loved my country I returned not only to die in it, but with it."

Belief in your myth and madness are not enough. In fact King Sebastian almost gives madness a bad name.

An interesting restoration project is underway in the cloister of the monastery. Five hundred years of what the information boards call "biological colonization" and most of us call mold are being removed by various techniques, including lasers. The visitor can clearly see just how far the restoration has progressed. The restored stone is luminous and golden. I think of monasteries as being grim; but in its day Jeronimos most certainly was not and perhaps soon will not be again.

The Museu de Marinha is fascinating but almost too big, or perhaps we approached it at the end of a too long day.

Located in the West Wing of Jeronimos Monastery, the main collection is housed in two large halls, progressing from early navigators to the twentieth century, and includes artifacts, ship models, navigation instruments, and paintings. In addition to the voyages known to the world, there is much from Portuguese colonial history with which I, at least, was not familiar. One object that has remained in my mind is a flag carried ashore in an assault on a German position in Africa during the Great War. Small X's have been sewn over holes made by machine gun bullets. I counted thirty in one section of the folded flag and can only wonder at the fate of the man carrying it. Perhaps he held it high and kept his head low.

On another day we visited the national art museum, the Museu de Arte Antiga, which is located about half way between Belém and the city center, within sight of THE HAWKE OF TUONELA's berth. The building was originally a seventeenth-century palace, acquired by the Marquês de Pombal. A monastery destroyed in the 1755 earthquake occupied the site before the palace and its only surviving remnant, the chapel, is a part of the museum.

Everywhere in Lisbon, everywhere in Portugal, one is confronted with the Catholic Church. Churches, cathedrals, monasteries, and the names of saints are ubiquitous, despite Portugal having banned religious orders in 1834. Nowhere is the influence of the church more apparent than in the national museum where the visitor passes through room after room after room of Madonnas and child, Christs crucified, and saints. Sebastian with arrows and Catherine beheaded seem to be particular Por-

Ruins of Carmelite Church, Lisbon, destroyed by the earthquake of 1755

71

Carol with resident cats, Carmelite Church, Lisbon

tuguese favorites. For hundreds of years, that was all anyone with any artistic talent or aspiration painted or sculpted. After a while, or perhaps from the beginning, they all seem the same, and it was with some relief that we came across the first daring portraits of people, man finally turning his gaze on man in the Renaissance.

My favorite paintings in the museum were a view of Lisbon from across the river of historical rather than artistic merit and one of Hieronymus Bosch's patented nightmares, "The Temptations of Saint Anthony." Mr. Bosch's saints do not look like anyone else's.

Hills rise on both sides of central Lisbon.

To the east is the old Moorish quarter capped by the Castle de São Jorge. To the west are the cobbled streets of the Barrio Alto and the Chiado, home of the statues of Camões and Pessoa.

The best views of the castle are from the Miradouro de San Pedro de Alcantara and from the café at the top of the Elevador de Santa Justa, a steel filigree designed by a disciple of Monsieur Eiffel, which is a pleasant place to stop for a drink.

The best views of the Barrio Alto and the Chiado are from the castle. Delicate stone ribs from the ruins of the Carmelite Church lace against the western skyline. The church was the largest in Lisbon when it was destroyed. Its congregation was crushed while attending mass when the earthquake of 1755 struck. A reconstruction project was halted first by lack of funds and then by the romantic attraction to ruins. To my eye the romantics were right. The remaining roofless walls and arches are strangely beautiful and evocative. And they are the home to stray cats, who have the run of the place, sun themselves on the warm stones, and reminded us of Shatters-the-reluctant-ship's-cat.

One weekend we did what many locals do and rode the train to Cascais, a beach resort ten miles west of Lisbon.

Like practically every place along the Portuguese coast, Cascais was originally a fishing village, and the fishermen have not yet been completely driven out. A marina was developed a few years ago, which is expensive by Portuguese standards and was, even in August, only half full. From a restaurant on a cliff overlooking the harbor we saw several boats at anchor and, although the harbor is completely open to the south, we found the place pretty enough so that we anchored ourselves there for a few days after leaving Lisbon.

With the tide with us when we left Doca da Alcantara, we raced downstream and covered the distance to the forts at the river mouth in less than one hour, five times faster than we had coming upstream on our arrival.

11 The Real World

In 1983 when I first sailed to Portugal—from England in
RESURGAM and from Suez via Malta in CHIDIOCK TICHBORNE II—
the only marina in the 250 miles between Lisbon and Gibraltar
was at Vilamoura midway along Portugal's Algarve coast.

In 2001 more than a dozen marinas were open along the same
stretch of water and more were under construction.

Although it would have been possible, we did not intend to
daysail all the way to Gibraltar, but our plan to stop somewhere
on the west coast before turning the corner at Cape Saint
Vincent ended in a fog bank two hours south of Cascais.

I have not been much troubled by fog on my voyages. Of
course it is prevalent in San Francisco, where I started sailing
which is one of the reasons I moved south to San Diego, and in
Maine.

During the first summer after Carol and I were married, after
sailing THE HAWKE OF TUONELA up from Florida, I cruised the
coast of Maine. I even saw it from time to time. Once I sat for
three days in a harbor a few miles from Camden in fog so thick
I could not see the bow from the cockpit, much less the rocky
shore thirty yards away. I listened to sailors determined to make
the most of their scheduled vacations work their way in each
afternoon, drop anchor, then leave the next morning for another
invisible harbor. While these were impressive feats of piloting, I
wondered what was the point.

The other memory I had of fog was my very first sail in
RESURGAM in 1983.

She was in a boatyard several miles up the River Orwell on
the east coast of England when I bought her. By leaving at noon

I could ride the tide south along the coast to Dover, catch the change there, and ride the next tide west to Brighton.

Bright sunshine when I left the boatyard disappeared within minutes of my entering the North Sea. On a boat which was new to me and where nothing yet fell easily to hand, I spent a long afternoon and night following the twenty meter curve on the depthsounder, which I had determined would keep me off the numerous, ominously named knocks and shoals to my west, and hopefully inside the numerous and ominous sounding ships I could hear to my east. I also used a Radio Direction Finder to get bearings on the beacons along the coast. With only moderate wind, I was startled to find those beacons flying past as the tide gave us eight to ten knots over the bottom. That was one of the few nights I have gone sleepless.

Off Portugal almost twenty years later, our situation was not so serious. Although all the shipping going to and from the Mediterranean was a few miles to our west, we had radar, GPS, and I knew THE HAWKE OF TUONELA so well I could sail her blindfolded. We could find our way into port if we had to, but I was more comfortable remaining at sea.

The fog was cold and for a few hours windless. We went from shorts and T-shirts to jeans, long-sleeved shirts, Polartec, and finally foulweather gear.

We powered, sailed, powered, sailed, and powered some more.

During the night some stars briefly appeared, along with the running lights of five ships a mile to the west. We tacked away from them. The stars and running lights disappeared. The following midmorning the fog lightened and finally burned off, revealing Cape Saint Vincent, the sheer promontory that is the southwest corner of Europe, a few miles ahead.

Cape Saint Vincent looks the way the corner of a continent should, a lighthouse above weathered cliffs, boldly jutting into the sea.

Cruising guides and pilot books warn of the acceleration of wind in the vicinity of the cape and advise sailors not to cut too close, but at noon on that calm day we motored a half mile off, while another boat taking advantage of the unusual conditions to get north passed even closer inside us.

Cape Saint Vincent is the westernmost of a triple set of headlands, the next and southernmost being Sagres, where Prince Henry—known as The Navigator, though he himself never navigated anything except perhaps his nation's destiny—settled and established a school, and then Atalaia.

If it had not still be been late August we might have gone into the new marina at Sagres, which is a favorite of many sailors we met, but we saw boats anchored in the unprotected roadstead and concluded that there was no room in the inn and continued on to Portimão, where I knew there was ample space to anchor inside the breakwaters.

The light seemed to change after we rounded Cape Saint Vincent, become warmer, yellower, and, although we were in fact being funneled toward the Straits of Gibraltar, we felt a sense of openness and space. Perhaps it was the knowledge that Europe lay to our north, but a new continent, Africa, was just over the horizon to the south.

A sailboat under power is an inefficient powerboat, but, sadly, that is what THE HAWKE OF TUONELA was as we powered in order to reach Portimão before sunset, and that is what she was to be for many miles to come. Between Cape Saint Vincent and the Guadiana River which is the border between Portugal and Spain we had only one hour of wind, and that was on the nose.

Portimão

When you arrive in a new harbor you have to reinvent the wheel and locate the necessities of life, from fresh water and food to perhaps diesel fuel, a telephone, post office and an Internet connection.

Portimão caused me to reevaluate what makes a good harbor because many of the necessities were not easy to locate or obtain, yet we sailed in for a night and left two weeks later, only occasionally bothering to wonder why we were so content.

The harbor is the half-mile wide estuary of the Rio Arade made into a good anchorage by two long breakwaters angling out from the shore. Portimão dates from Roman times, and is more than a mile inland on the west side of the river. With a population of 40,000 it rivals Faro as the largest city on the Algarve coast. A jumble of high-rise hotels at Praia da Rocha clutters the shoreline to the west. Midway between Praia da Rocha and Portimão is another new marina, which in 2001 was still significantly empty. And that is the secret of Portimão: West bad! East good!

First let me express a personal preference: even ignoring cost, I would rather be at anchor or on a mooring than in a marina. I own an anchor—actually three anchors—and I know how to use them. I have equipped THE HAWKE OF TUONELA to anchor, with bow roller, chain stopper, two snubbing lines, several rodes, the primary of which is 200 feet of 5⁄16-inch high test chain, and a manual anchor windlass. My aging back may cause me to go electric, but not yet.

At anchor a boat is alive, she swings with the wind, has better ventilation, more privacy, and better views from the cockpit. In addition, I just like having a moat between me and the world.

Inside the east breakwater at Portimão is a good anchorage in 12 to 20 feet of water off several small white sand beaches, backed and separated by reddish sandstone cliffs, the ruins of a Moorish fort, and the tiny fishing village of Ferragudo. A few restaurants are scattered at the base of the cliffs; but the clean, uncrowded beaches seem to be frequented mostly by locals, and tourism on the east side of the harbor is very subdued.

Landing the dinghy directly on the beach, we would carry it above high tide mark and walk the half mile to Ferragudo along the cliffs, past the fort and cypress trees that seemed Roman and houses with window boxes overflowing with flowers. From the cliffs there were fine views down at the anchorage.

At low tide we could walk the other direction from beach to beach and then climb a path to the lighthouse and views along the coast or walk out to the end of the breakwater.

From the cockpit of THE HAWKE OF TUONELA, people promenading on the opposite breakwater at sunset became a string of silhouetted hieroglyphs.

In a sign of the times Ferragudo has no supermarket, but does have a one-computer Internet connection and a handful of outdoor restaurants along an indentation where small fishing boats moor. Your guaranteed fresh sea food is grilled over open fires in modified 55 gallon drums.

Ferragudo also has a maze of steep footpaths paved with marble chips. Portugal is the world's second largest exporter of marble, and the rubble left from removing bigger blocks makes inexpensive surfacing.

From a distance Ferragudo is a cubist sculpture, and it is not surprising that Picasso, who was born in Málaga, a couple of hundred miles further east on the Iberian coast, was for a while a cubist. It was what he was seeing.

There was usually something pleasant or interesting to look at or watch on our side of Portimão.

In the early morning a solitary black dog ran along the beach, dashing into the water, far ahead of a solitary man; and colorfully painted one-man fishing boats dotted the harbor around us.

Later there were a few wind surfers and, something we had not seen before, kite-surfing in which the surfer is propelled at startling speed by a parafoil.

From the cockpit we watched the day trip boats go out and return. One is an imitation caravel, from the great age of discovery; another a bright yellow imitation mobile home.

Two of the big sailing cruise ships entered the harbor. They were impressive. And would have been even more so had we ever seen them sail.

Coastal fishing boats chugged past in clouds of seagulls.

Three times we left the east side of the harbor and went west for logistical reasons. Once we raised anchor and went to the marina fuel dock, where we took on fuel, which we did not need, and water, which we did. The people at the marina were pleasant and helpful, but a good anchorage is tough competition. Portimão is the only harbor in Portugal I know of where one has the choice, and usually ten to fifteen boats swung around THE HAWKE OF TUONELA.

And twice I rowed to Praia da Rocha for groceries. A hypermarket is a taxi ride away, but a useful medium size market can be found off Praia da Rocha's crass main street. The beach on that side facing the ocean is enormously long and wide, and clusters of sun umbrellas stretch forever.

The wind kicked up during the row back, perhaps to twenty knots. In an Avon Redstart it was hard work, and a jet ski with two young Portuguese men came out from the shore and generously offered us a tow. I thanked them, but said, "Not yet."

Vilamoura

It has become fashionable to hate the big 1,000-boat marina at Vilamoura. Cruisers uniformly told us how much they disliked the place and how glad they were to leave as quickly as possible.

Vilamoura is Portugal's most expensive marina and it certainly has changed since I first docked there in 1983. We paid $26 a night. But Vilamoura is well organized, well run—each day a staff member came by the boat to offer assistance with any problems—and has exceptional facilities, including the nicest showers we have seen in any marina, and free Internet service. And at least on our dock off to one side of the basin, it was quiet.

Having said that, the place is almost unrecognizable since my last visit in 1989. In what is reputed to be the biggest resort complex in Europe, the entire area is filled with hotels, residences, and a casino. I became lost just trying to find the way to the beach, which in the 1980s was bordered only by shacks built by Angolan refugees. Some of those shacks, now mostly abandoned, are still there, a narrow necklace of ruins in prime real estate. The marina, surrounded by restaurants and shops, has itself become a tourist destination, with thousands of visitors strolling around each day.

In addition to curiosity to see the changes—Carol had flown

back from there to join me in Florida in 1994—we stopped at Vilamoura to complete some chores, including laundry, grocery shopping and cooking gas tank refill. Lisbon, Vilamoura, and Gibraltar, are the only places where it is possible, but by no means certain, that U.S. tanks can be filled.

While living aboard in Boston, one of our ten-pound aluminum tanks generally lasted two months. Because at sea our dinners are freeze dry food, which only requires heating two cups of water, and because low prices encouraged us to eat ashore frequently in Portugal; since leaving Boston a tank had lasted three months and one week.

Although we had to wait an extra day for the essential man to come to work, the chandlery in Vilamoura filled our tank routinely.

Coiled on the floor of the chandlery, half hidden by a rack of foulweather gear, I found the solution to what had been our only serious problem: a long length of head hose. Although I replaced the twenty-year-old original only a year earlier, the new head discharge hose had become exceedingly malodorous. Exceedingly. Words do not suffice. The hose in the chandlery was 40mm, the close equivalent of our 1½" fittings, and after taking some measurements, I bought it and spent a morning in the pleasant task of replacing the existing evil. At least for a while we wouldn't be buying air freshener by the case.

We arrived in Vilamoura at about noon local time, which is five hours ahead of the U.S. East Coast, on September 11, 2001. While doing the laundry that afternoon, we noticed a crowd gathering in front of a café television. Portuguese television was carrying CNN live and so we saw the events of the day almost from the beginning. We were the only U.S. boat on our dock, and people from England, Scotland, Germany, and Portugal expressed their shock and sympathy. I have never before as an American been the object of other peoples' pity. It was an odd and unsettling feeling.

Culatra

A few miles east of Vilamoura the Algarve coast, which since Cape Saint Vincent has been rust and beige sandstone cliffs broken by river mouths and beaches, becomes a sand barrier island in the form of a twenty mile long V. Near the angle of the V is a channel into a wide shallow lagoon. On the north side of the lagoon are the cities of Faro, with a population of 40,000, and Olhão, with another 15,000.

Much of the lagoon dries at low tide, but there are still several anchorages. Most boats, usually about a dozen while we were there, swing off a tiny village on the Island of Culatra, which forms the east arm of the V.

About twenty years ago the entire area was designated a nature reserve, apparently to prevent tourist development. This is the Parque Natural da Ria Formosa. In Portuguese formosa means beautiful, but it isn't.

When we first entered we felt the need for solitude and continued a mile past the village to a sand spit near the end of the island.

It happened to be a Saturday and a few families had come from the mainland in powerboats to picnic on the beach, but they left by dark. From the water, for a while, it looked pleasant and pristine. But then the Great Garbage Island drifted down upon us.

With more than 50,000 people on the far shore and, as we later learned, no trash collection at the fishing village, as well as no electricity or public water, until the late 1990s, a tremendous amount of trash has found its way into the lagoon and been compacted by the tides, along with sea weed and chunks of wood, into a long serpentine mess that lazily oozed past us east on the ebb and west on the flood. And the following day, when I went ashore, I found that the beach is littered with trash at the high water mark. Even well away from the water are burial mounds of plastic water bottles, apparently taken from the village and dumped in the years before public trash collection.

Like any harbor that significantly uncovers at low tide, there are inevitable smells. But these tides also create an industry. 80% of Portugal's mollusk exports come from the lagoon, and in the hours around low tide people appear, wading, walking, digging, where a few hours earlier a sheet of water extended miles to the mainland.

Before moving on we joined the boats off the village for a day and went ashore. The village is tiny and probably the most authentic still in existence, even with recent amenities such as television satellite dishes and frequent ferry service to the mainland. But what we found most memorable is not authentic, but imported.

From our first anchorage we had seen masts sprouting from the sand. Ashore at the village, we decided to investigate, and after climbing over some dunes, came upon a scene from Robinson Crusoe.

In a mud flat cove about fifty yards across is a collection of boats—I resist "graveyard"—upon which a community of people live year round, never going anywhere, except up and down on the tide, taking the ground twice a day, some never fully afloat.

Now I understand not having money. I have twice lost everything I owned in the world. But I don't understand choosing to stay in such a place, which is smelly and unattractive, and where, as one man who has been there for years told us, winter storms slam boats on the bottom with every wave. One vessel, he said with a wry smile, pancaked so much the owner had to cut new shrouds.

The cove is a curiosity. One of the extremes of boat life. Or rather life in boats. And as such is perhaps worth a visit and contemplation.

Alcoutim

In fables there is a great beauty who is guarded by dragons.

In Portugal there is a great beauty, Alcoutim, and she is guarded by dragons in the forms of a bridge, a bar at a river mouth, and tides.

The bridge worried me most, but it proved chimerical. What worried me was not the bridge as much as four words in the cruising guide: "thought to be about", as in "clearance thought to be about 20 meters."

By my calculations THE HAWKE OF TUONELA requires 18 meters of clearance. As we sailed east I kept looking up at the masthead and visualizing the possible damage: masthead instruments; light; Windex; furling gear; rigging; the mast itself. It was unthinkable. And so I started asking sailors we met if they had been up the Guadiana River, which separates Portugal and Spain. All of those who replied affirmatively had masts shorter than ours, but thought we could make it at low tide. One said, "Just go at it steady." I still don't understand how bridge height is increased by a boat's rate of acceleration. Another assured us categorically, "No problem." Coming from a man who lived in one of the wrecks at Culatra and did not even know what size boat we have, this was not reassuring.

A Portuguese sailor passed a message to us through an intermediary who shouted, "He says it is 24 meters." But then added, "But I think it is only about 20."

Before reaching the bridge, which is four miles up stream, a sailor has to get across the river bar, which is marked but like all river bars shifts position. The advice from both the cruising guide and a Portuguese publication about marinas is to enter only in good weather and the half flood or above tide. Following this advice we had a minimum of 14 feet of water and no problems going in, though our exit under less favorable conditions was sufficiently rough that we acknowledge its validity.

Near the mouth of the river are the Portuguese town of Villa Real and the Spanish town of Ayamonte. Both have marinas. The one at Villa Real has a narrow entrance which requires an immediate 90° turn to starboard to the reception dock and is subject to strong currents. The entrance at Ayamonte is less harrowing. The advice for Villa Real is to maneuver only at slack water. We powered by and saw an accident waiting to happen and continued on to anchor on the Ayamonte side a mile below

THE HAWKE OF TUONELA and Alcoutim, Portugal, as seen from Sanlucar, Spain

the bridge. And that is the problem with the Guadiana. You want to cross the bar at the half flood, but you want to go under the bridge at low tide, and if you want to go into the marina at Villa Real you should do so at slack water. In late September, throw in a couple of early fall low pressure systems, and we were stuck for two days anchored off Ayamonte both coming and going.

As soon as I saw the bridge it ceased to worry me. Or did except for the last few seconds before we reached it. If your mast is no longer than ours, you will have clearance within an hour of low tide. How much clearance? Well, the cruising guide says "thought to be . . ."

We headed up river on a blustery, showery afternoon on the trailing edge of a low, planning once we were past the bridge to anchor if conditions became too unpleasant. Although rain fell intermittently on the brown hills around us, we continued chugging our way for twenty miles north, past groves of olive trees and a handful of tiny villages, until we came around the final bend and found the beauty that rendered the trials insignificant.

The guidebooks use words like "gemlike" and "unspoiled," and it is.

A man on a powerboat who had been there for six months called it "paradise," which might be a stretch. But then it might not be. The place is that lovely and serene.

Twin villages, Alcoutim on the Portuguese side and Sanlucar on the Spanish, face one another across a hundred yards of water. A thousand people are said to live in Alcoutim, but it seems smaller.

Both villages have public docks to which boats can tie for a slight charge: at Alcoutim it was less than $3 a day, including water and electricity. Alcoutim also has laid seven free moorings, one of which we picked up. A few boats were at anchor above and below the villages.

Both villages are of the requisite whitewashed, red tile roof buildings, except for one rebel in Sanlucar who has painted his house mauve. In this case conformity would have been better.

Both are built on hills, have churches which, because Spain is one hour ahead of Portugal, compete each hour ringing different times, both have Moorish forts, the one in Sanlucar higher and dominating the countryside. The Moors were driven from Portugal hundreds of years earlier than from Spain.

Sanlucar has a Don Quixote windmill. And on a hillside just south of the village, a pastoral tableau: four horses, two white, two black, usually stand beneath a group of trees, and a flock of sheep, accompanied by one goat, all with bells around their necks, graze in a routine that brings them down to the river at sunset. There is also a donkey, never seen but frequently heard, and roosters, who perhaps confused by the differing church bells, crow at odd hours.

In the middle of the river, we could choose which country we wanted to row to. We ate ashore at Alcoutim, but shopped for groceries in Sanlucar.

One morning I awoke thinking I had left the radio on in the main cabin, but when I got up to shut it off I discovered that it was a radio ashore in the next country. I went to the companionway, as I did each morning we were there, to look around and see if the place really was as pretty as I remembered. Each morning it was.

A road down to Villa Real runs along the river on the Portuguese side, but the sight of a car, or the twice a day bus, was rare. Traffic is so light that a café sets up tables on the only street—though that is too imposing a word—leading away from the town center. Once while we were sipping a cup of coffee there, the lady at the next table stopped a bread truck inching its way past and gave the driver a few coins, apparently taking the opportunity to pay her bill.

We spent hours on deck, just looking around.

One afternoon we happened to observe a sure nomination for the world's worst docking. A German ketch with a two-man crew squeezed onto the end of the Alcoutim dock. The man at the bow threw a line to the owner of the boat ahead, who hurried to help in kindness or self-defense, but the crew member simply held onto his end of the line and was almost pulled into the river when the other end was secured to the dock. Simultaneously the helmsman calmly stepped ashore with a stern line which he tied to a cleat, but whose other end was not in any way connected to the boat. Another good reason to prefer moorings and anchoring.

Even in Alcoutim the outer world intruded. One day we were eating lunch in a restaurant frequented by Portuguese workmen. A television in one corner was on but ignored until when the national news came on at 1:00 p.m, the room fell suddenly silent as everyone stopped eating and turned to the screen. Only when there was no news of a retaliatory strike or another terrorist attack, did people resume their lives.

In late September the weather between lows was perfect: sunny, highs around 80°, low humidity, and we were tempted to linger; but two long-standing October appointments in Gibraltar compelled motion. Those and the sun, which had left the hemisphere. Even if it did not seem to be, it was fall, and we intended to follow the sun across the Equator.

When in the past in some exotic port I have been asked, "But what do you do in the real world?" I have replied, "But *this* is the real world." Now I no longer knew. Is the real world Alcoutim? Or is it the destruction of the World Trade Center in Manhattan? Logic says both. But my mind struggled to reconcile the two.

12 Gibraltar

I almost died once in the Straits of Gibraltar, and another time my life turned there.

I almost died in August of 1983 when I was caught by the east wind known as the levanter on the passage from Malta to Vilamoura in CHIDIOCK TICHBORNE II.

In the morning I sailed past Gibraltar in light wind. I could easily have gone in, but didn't. Though the passage had been slow, as any passage is in the light and fluky summer Mediterranean winds, both the boat and I were in good shape and I wanted to get to Vilamoura, where RESURGAM waited.

About midday half-way through the straits and a half-mile off the sheer Spanish hills falling into the water, the levanter came as suddenly and unexpectedly as any wind I have known.

In the open sea there is almost always warning. During the day clouds and squall lines can be seen approaching. At sunset I examine the sky and while I have sometimes had false positives and thought we might have trouble during the night and slept lightly on guard against weather that did not develop, I never recall a false negative, of thinking that everything was all right and then experiencing serious weather before dawn.

But not near the land, and particularly not near big bodies of water like the Great Lakes and the Med, where pressure moves quickly from land to water and back again. Especially not in a place like the Straits of Gibraltar, where water and wind are funneled in the eight mile gap between the mountains of Spain and the mountains of Morocco in a great, dramatically appropriate, western end to the classical world.

In CHIDIOCK TICHBORNE II I was caught with full sail up when the wind increased from less than ten knots to over forty in seconds.

Full sail was only 130 square feet, divided into three sails, 30 square feet each in a furling jib and a mizzen and 70 in a loose footed main.

I did not sail CHIDIOCK as much as wear her, sitting and sleeping on the grated floorboards, beside or under the tiller. At sea I used jib sheet to tiller self-steering, but close to land I steered myself. At the instant the wind increased fortunately I had the tiller in my left hand. Simultaneously I felt the wind against my skin and the power of the little yawl accelerating through the water.

The wind, which had been coming from the sheer land to starboard, now blew from almost dead astern, just slightly on the port quarter. I threw my weight to that side of the boat, changed hands on the tiller, and eased the mainsheet. I would have lowered the main, but I could not let go of the tiller long enough to get to where the halyard was belayed. The distance was not great. Not more than six feet. After all the whole boat was only eighteen feet long. It wouldn't have taken more than seconds. Perhaps only two or three. But I knew the boat would capsize before I could do it.

CHIDIOCK TICHBORNE was an extraordinarily well built and good sailing little boat. She displaced less than 900 pounds and had a centerboard, which was at that moment part way down, but she was never intended to get up on a plane. I don't know that technically she did. I do know that as it had thousands of miles earlier in a fifty-knot storm near Tahiti, her boat speed indicator pegged at the maximum ten-knot reading as we blasted past the rocky Spanish coast.

The wind came up so suddenly that for a while there were no waves. But after half an hour or so they began to build. They were not high, only two or three feet, but they were steep and close together, and CHIDIOCK TICHBORNE began to roll as she surfed down them, her bow wave arching high above her 14-inch freeboard.

I steered small, trying to keep the little yawl in the groove, hoping for a lull that would enable me to let go of the tiller long enough to drop the main, which was on what is known as a sliding gunter rig. This means that the upper part of the sail was attached to a gaff that was a vertical extension of the mast. Its weight would automatically cause the sail to fall if I could just unbelay the halyard. But a lull never came. Instead the levanter increased to over fifty knots as the strait narrowed and our course converged on the fast approaching point of land jutting out at Tarifa.

I did not think I could jibe with the main up without capsizing. I wasn't going to try until I had to. Even if I was thrown clear, there was no place to get ashore, only waves smashing against rock.

People ran down to the point as I approached. Waving their arms and yelling for me to steer away. As usual when people yell, they didn't understand the problem.

I was sailing by the lee, my eyes moving from the leech of the main to the rocky headland before us and back again, feeling the main collapse, steering up until it filled, which pointed us more toward the land and caused more shouts, which barely reached me, then off again.

In the last few seconds, the people ashore fell silent. None of us knew if I was going to make it. Vaguely I saw them on the upper edge of my vision, standing gape mouthed, as CHIDIOCK TICHBORNE and I blasted past with whole feet to spare. Then they broke into yells again, presumably of congratulations. I was too busy sailing and looking for isolated rocks to glance back.

While the land immediately receded toward the northwest and I was in a few seconds safe from running aground, I could not let go of the tiller long enough to lower the main until we reached the shelter of Trafalgar Point some twenty miles further on. We covered the distance in ninety minutes.

Five years and a circumnavigation later my life turned literally at Gibraltar as in the small grocery store at Marina Quay, I saw Jill collapse at the far end of the aisle. In slow motion she pirouetted, one arm lifted, hand raised, fingers curved, falling, spinning slowly out of control in a moment that began a sequence of events in which our lives spun out of control for a while.

I recalled these memories as we powered past Tarifa, somewhat further off than I was in CHIDIOCK, on a sunny Sunday afternoon. The good wind when we exited the Guadiana the preceding day had died during the night, and rather than sit I had turned on the engine. I am told that diesels like to be used. Mine usually isn't. But we used more fuel from Lisbon to Gibraltar than we did from Boston to Lisbon. So I hoped the Yanmar was happy. It sounded happy.

A small whirlpool formed in the middle of a patch of small spiky waves leaping up like those in Japanese prints where the west-going tide overflowed the constant east-heading current of water being drawn into the Med to replace that lost by evaporation.

Beyond it was the procession of ships moving through the straits and beyond them the sere brown mountains of Morocco.

I had been rereading Herodotus, who mentions almost as a footnote what was probably the greatest voyage into the unknown ever made.

Later I looked up the exact quote. "Libya" was the Greek word for Africa, not just the single country by that name today.

As for Libya, we know it to be surrounded on all sides by the sea, except where it is attached to Asia. This discovery was first made by Necos, the Egyptian king, who on desisting from the canal which he had begun between the Nile and the Arabian Gulf, sent to sea a number of ships manned by Phoenicians, with orders to make for the Pillars of Hercules, and return to Egypt through them, and by the Mediterranean. The Phoenicians took their departure from Egypt by way of the Erythraean Sea, and so sailed into the southern ocean. When autumn came, they went ashore, wherever they might happen to be, and having sown a tract of land with corn, waited until the grain was fit to cut. Having reaped it, they again set sail; and thus it came to pass that two whole years went by, and it was not till the third year that they doubled the Pillars of Hercules, and made good their voyage home. On their return, they declared—I for my part do not believe them, but perhaps others may—that in sailing round Libya they had the sun upon their right hand. In this was the extent of Libya first discovered.

I tried to imagine them coming through the straits more than two thousand years ago, hugging the far shore, joyous to be back into the known world. There would have been many fewer people and many more animals then. I've sailed around perhaps three quarters of the continent on various voyages, though usually further offshore than I expect the Phoenicians would have been. I think it must have been hard for them to leave the Garden of Eden around Table Mountain, and I think they would have known great despair in the fog along the coast of the Namib Desert, and then again when they had to follow the bulge of Africa west. What sailors they must have been; what men to have endured and survived. I would have loved to have been one of them.

That the sun was on their right was exactly where it would have been during much of the voyage, despite Herodotus' skepticism. But then probably no one believed most of the stories they had to tell when they got home.

I like to picture them years after the voyage, sitting in a tavern along the waterfront of their small home ports, gazing out at the sea, remembering, knowing that they had seen things no one around them could even imagine.

Carol and I reached Gibraltar just before dark, tied to the Customs dock, expecting to spend the night there, but found officers still on duty, who quickly cleared us, and then found Gibraltar in October almost as crowded as had been Horta in June, but this was to be expected. October is the month of migration for charter boats that summer in the Med and winter in the Caribbean, and, again, there were two rallies in port. Or to be exact one new round the world rally starting from there and dozens of boats on their way to the start of the ARC in the Canaries.

We left the Customs dock, powered around the single airport landing strip that juts out into the bay, and anchored in the narrow strip of water between Gibraltar and Spain for the night.

The next morning I rowed ashore, ran afoul of various officials who told me I couldn't land here and shouldn't go there, and others who told me the opposite. When I finally made my way through the maze ashore, I was told by all three marinas that there was no space, but that something might open up.

While I like to be at anchor, Gibraltar is not the place for it. The designated anchorage is exceedingly inconvenient, without access even to a water tap. We considered moving around the breakwater fifty yards north into Spain, but fortunately a space opened at Marina Quay that afternoon. We were very glad to have it, even though we were almost cremated by the afterburner of a British fighter jet taking off as we shifted the boat. That is a danger the ancient Phoenicians did not have to face.

Two clouds define Gibraltar, one physical, one political.

Physically the rock is big enough and isolated enough so that it forms its own mini-climate. Particularly in the winter, a cloud hangs over Gibraltar, causing the narrow strip of land on the west side where 30,000 Gibraltarians squeeze together to be overcast and chilly, when a quarter mile north Spain is in bright sunshine.

Politically Gibraltar lives under the cloud of the Treaty of Utrecht of 1713, in which Spain ceded the area to England at the end of The War of the Spanish Succession.

British and Spanish diplomats spend endless negotiations about the exact terms of the treaty, as though anything a government says can be counted on beyond its immediate advantage, much less three hundred years.

Both Britain and Spain would like Gibraltar to become Spanish, though Spain has no intention of giving Ceuta, which it holds on the Moroccan side of the Strait, back to Morocco. The problem is that the Gibraltarians don't want to be Spanish, even though many of them are.

Spain tries to put pressure on Gibraltar in various ways. At times it has closed the border completely, the primary effect of which was to increase poverty at La Linga, the town on the Spanish side, many of whose residents work daily in Gibraltar and became unemployed. Spain has managed to block most air travel to and from Gibraltar, and the only flights in 2001 were to and from the U.K, which affected us because one of our reasons for being there was for Carol to fly back to Boston for the official opening of the medical research center at the University of Massachusetts in Worcester.

The other reason we were there was to link up with some of Carol's friends who were vacationing in Europe.

In the past Gibraltar was a good place to get boat work done, but now other facilities exist in the region. Fortunately we did not need any services, for everything was backlogged and sailors who did need repairs or maintenance faced waiting lists and long delays.

The chandleries were less well stocked than they had been in the past. They seemed to have adopted a policy of reducing inventory by taking orders to be filled from the U.K.

Carol had wanted to see Gibraltar, and we saw the sights with her friends in a day: the apes, the view from the cable car, a walk along Main Street with shops full of items that are not bargains, the changing of the guard at Government House, a full moon that silvered the north face of the rock.

Food is not usually important to me. I like good food if I can get it, but I can live on my usual passage food of uncooked oatmeal, trail mix and powdered milk, and a freeze-dried dinner without complaint. Yet one of the special pleasures of foreign ports had become our long lunches. In Gibraltar we never did find a good restaurant. The food was at best mediocre and generally more expensive than in other places we visited. You don't have to look at the flag to know Gibraltar is British.

The best thing about Gibraltar was watching the passing parade of superyachts. Gibraltar in October may be the best place in the world to see them. One hundred footers are common, power and sail, anchored stern-to to the outside of the marina; the very biggest anchored out with the tankers in the bay. Yachts of 70 or 80 feet that would normally dominate a harbor become mundane, probably much to the chagrin of their owners.

Gibraltar is one of those places, like the Panama Canal, that are worth seeing once, but this was my third time. Carol saw what there was to see; her friends visited; she flew to Boston for the building opening; and when she returned, we were ready to go, having remained almost a month in a place where two days would have been enough.

The Green Sea of Darkness

The wind was howling around the Rock at near gale force as we raised anchor on the grey, gloomy dawn of November 3, and the straits were forecast to be rough; but these were localized conditions, and with the tide with us we expected to have better weather within an hour or two.

We were again anchored on the north side of the airport, having been towed away from Marina Quay the preceding afternoon by obliging marina staff.

There are no doubt many reasons to try to sail in the Med. As a philosophy student and as a reader, one of my early dreams was to sail the isles of Greece, but I never have and I doubt I ever will. I think I am too late for Greece, and other places attract me more.

There are two very good reasons not to sail the Med. The first is that you can't really. In the summer there isn't much wind. Although I did trudge the length of the sea in the engineless CHIDIOCK TICHBORNE, that was a triumph of endurance and a trial of patience. I spent most of another summer at Puerto Banus on Spain's Costa del Sol and can recall perhaps one or two days of sailing wind a month. The Med is for powerboats and we were tired of powering.

The second reason not to sail the Med is Med-style marinas where there are no side docks between boats, only long piers to which you tie either bow or stern with an anchor or line to a buoy at the other end of the boat to keep you more or less perpendicular. Less, often much less, when strong wind comes from abeam and accordions an entire row of boats. The only advantage to such an arrangement is decreased construction costs to the marina developer.

In Gibraltar we were wedged bow to the dock between two other boats near the office building and when it came time to leave the wind was blowing strong from astern. With no room to maneuver, we had to be towed clear to go out and anchor for an early start the following morning.

Carol started the engine and powered forward to put some slack in the chain as I winched it in. A few other sailboats and two fishing trawlers were around us. We were in 20 feet of water. When I felt the anchor come free I signaled to Carol, who let the wind spin THE HAWKE OF TUONELA and speed us along a corridor between a dozen ships anchored in the bay, waiting their turn to unload in Gibraltar or at the oil refinery in Spain.

By the time we cleared the ships I had secured the anchor and cleaned the foredeck and made my way back to the cockpit, where I unfurled a small amount of jib. We cut the engine and continued making six to seven knots, still in the lee of the looming Rock.

We had just made one of the two major turns of the voyage.

So far our course had been east. Corresponding latitudes do not always have corresponding climates and, though it is difficult to equate them, Gibraltar is only six degrees south of Boston. Now we were headed south, actually southwest because of the bulge of Africa and the wind patterns of the world, initially for Dakar for bureaucrats and curiosity and then Brazil, before turning east again for South Africa and eventually Australia. In the process we would go more than half the distance back west that we had just sailed from Boston. Boston's longitude is about 71°W. Gibraltar's 5°W. And Rio de Janeiro's 43°W.

That seems indirect, but it is the way the wind blows. We would be riding the edges of the two great wheels of wind that rotate clockwise in the northern hemisphere and counterclockwise in the southern, passing through the doldrums just north of the equator from one to the other, and then following the flow of wind around the southern wheel to Brazil and later, on its far rim, to Cape Town.

Choppy waves built as we moved beyond the Rock. Another levanter, but not as strong as the one I had experienced in CHID-IOCK TICHBORNE, and there is something to be said for having 14,000 pounds of boat and 40 inches of freeboard between you and the ocean instead of 900 pounds and 14 inches.

With the jib furled to the point that we probably didn't have much more sail set than that I had been trapped into carrying on CHIDIOCK, Carol and I sailed quickly through the narrowest part of the straits—though not as quickly as I did in the little yawl—and were soon under blue skies.

There are places in the world where shipping lanes become freeways. We had seen this off Cape Saint Vincent, and years earlier I had seen it just south of Sri Lanka where all the shipping between the Malacca Straits and Suez forms two lanes of traffic heading in opposite directions so solid that I had to heave to and wait for a break to cross.

Gibraltar was the same, only more so.

Coming from Portugal we had stayed north of the shipping, now we looked both ways, calculated speed, distance and gaps between ships, of which there were always a half dozen visible in both directions—those heading east throwing huge sprays of water over their bows as they powered into the wind and waves—and made our move. After getting across the outbound shipping, we sailed between the lanes for almost a half an hour before we could get through the inbound lane to the brown coast of Africa.

We ate lunch in the cockpit, looking into the port of Tangiers. I wouldn't have minded stopping. Everyplace is worth seeing once and Tangiers is certainly an evocative name, but we had thousands of miles to sail before the onset of the southern winter. Long ago I learned that you can't see everything, no matter how many times you sail around the world, and it is enough if you enjoy what you do see.

Beyond Tangiers, the coast began to fall away to the southwest and we followed it. Later that afternoon, when the shipping had spread out, we crossed through two northbound lanes, one heading to the Med, the other on to Northern Europe, without much difficulty and sought safety for the night further out to sea.

The following morning found us beating against a twenty-knot southwest wind, a deteriorating forecast with two lows forming, one directly ahead of us in the Canary Islands and another further north in the Atlantic, when not for the first and unfortunately not for the last time, the electrical system went out.

I checked the cables and all the connections without finding the cause of the problem. We had no lights, no instruments, no way to start the engine, and until I figured out how to bypass the solenoid switch to the propane tanks, no way to light the stove, though we did have a one-burner alcohol stove as back up.

While we were 140 miles from Gibraltar, we were only 90 miles south of Vilamoura. I knew that I could sail into the marina there under any conditions and tie up at the long reception dock or drop an anchor, although we couldn't make it before sunset. I didn't know what we would find in Dakar. With 20 knots on the nose, which would be astern if we turned, it was an easy decision. I pulled on the Monitor control lines, eased the sheets, and we headed north.

Conditions deteriorated during the day. The sky became completely overcast. Rain fell intermittently. And the wind backed, turning our broad reach into a beam reach into a close reach, until by nightfall in near zero visibility in heavy rain, we were close-hauled. I thought unpleasant thoughts until unexpectedly a cabin light came on. I flipped a few switches on the electrical panel. Everything was working. I didn't know why it happened or how long it would last, but the wind was now wrong for Portugal and I didn't really want to go back.

We turned again, having wasted most of a day, and headed for Dakar.

From the BBC we learned that the two lows were joining to form a giant storm. For two days we made slow progress southwest while covering a thousand miles up and down as we beat into a wind that had changed again. Fortunately the center of the gale was far away and passing well to the north of us. By the time it reached twenty knots it was blowing from astern, and THE HAWKE OF TUONELA sailed easily under a scrap of jib.

The gale carried us to within sight of the Canary Islands and my sixtieth birthday.

During it, we passed unseen Cape Brojodor, the merest excuse of a cape, completely unnoticeable on a modern chart of the African coast, but in its time more feared than Cape Horn is today. Brojodor stopped the Portuguese for a generation. Seamen refused to go beyond it, into what they called "a green sea of darkness" from which no ship could return. Foul currents, storms, sea monsters, an ocean that steamed and boiled. If they had read their Herodotus, they would have known that the Phoenicians had successfully come up from the south on their clockwise circumnavigation of Africa almost two thousand years earlier. But then Herodotus was not much known in fifteenth century Europe, and probably few of them could read at all. Finally in 1434 one captain, Gil Eannes, did venture beyond Brojodor, returned to tell the tale, and became a national hero.

November 11, our eighth day out of Gibraltar, saw us 70 miles west of Cape Brojodor and about the same south of the Canary Island of Fuerteventura. Our weather was clearing, but the BBC reported that overnight the now distant center of the storm had caused flooding, destruction and death in Algiers.

I was pleased to be at sea with Carol on my sixtieth birthday. I remembered being in New Zealand on my way back to Cape Horn on my fiftieth, but couldn't recall any other of my new decade birthdays. My fifties had been a trial, if largely of my own making, with a growing acceptance that parts of my life were not going to be as I had once dreamed. That I was at sea that day, heading out, was proof that I had endured if not prevailed, and that I had lasted much longer than anyone, including me, had ever expected. I was where I wanted to be.

Three hundred miles north of Dakar the night most improbably lit up. We were seventy miles off the coast of Mauritania, where the Sahara meets the sea, one of the poorest and emptiest countries in the world. At first I thought we were sailing into a field of offshore oil platforms, but the light came from a huge fishing fleet. We had not seen any other vessels during the day, but we saw fishing boats including big processing ships the following day, and their lights a second night as well.

We slowed down that night, even earlier than usual to time our arrival off Cape Verde, within whose fishhook shape lies Dakar, for dawn.

Cape Verde's flashing lighthouse became visible around midnight, as well as the running lights of substantial shipping, which cuts close to this westernmost point of Africa.

Seas built and became choppy as we sailed just offshore. Dawn revealed a sprawling city of mostly low buildings, dwarfed by several large mosques. Except for a few hills, the land was flat as far as the eye could see.

We had been advised by the only sailor I knew who had been to Dakar not to enter the commercial port, which has no place for yachts, but to proceed a few miles further east to the anchorage off the yacht clubs, from which it is permitted to taxi back into the city for official clearance.

A cluster of masts in a cove just west of the city center confused us. That was not where the yacht clubs were supposed to be, and I wondered if my information was out of date. Deciding to continue on, we lowered and furled the sails, powered outside of the island of Gorée, dodged several native pirogues, and were pleased to see more masts in the distance.

Dropping anchor outside of them in fifteen feet of muddy water, we pumped up the dinghy and rowed to Africa.

14 Goats and Groundnuts

If I were a goat I don't know that I would choose to live in Dakar. Life for goats is too hard there. As it is for people.

I thought this about goats every time we rode a taxi through a traffic circle whose cratered surface had been torn up by trucks until it looked as though it had been bombed and saw the same herd of goats eking out a living by eating whatever falls from the trucks. They grazed in the midst of the traffic, which flowed around them, bumpers, horns, exhaust fumes, inches away. Still we never saw a dead goat on the roadside, so perhaps it is safer than it looks.

I thought life in Senegal is too hard for people all the time.

Senegal's economy is based on groundnuts—peanuts to Americans. Senegal has excellent roasted groundnuts. Perhaps the best we have ever tasted. We found them for sale at thousands of stalls and vendors along the crowded streets, as well as in shops and stores. Small plates of them appeared as appetizers in restaurants and bars. They were mostly what fell from the trucks to nourish the goats. But still an economy based on groundnuts is, well, peanuts.

Fishing and tourism lag far behind, and the fishing is being depleted by the foreign fleets, mostly from Spain, we had seen off Mauritania, who plunder the waters of west African countries that do not have the means to protect their own accepted international limits.

Tourism is mostly from France, a vestige of colonial days, and in 2001 was slowly recovering from a decline caused by political disturbances in the early 1990s. Certainly, except for the day we rode the ferry to the island of Gorée, we saw few other

Contemplating a goat's life. Dakar, Senegal

tourists. Often we were the only customers in restaurants and the only foreign faces on the streets.

Those streets were filled with people. As a generalization the Senegalese are tall, fine boned, handsome and vibrantly dressed with every article of clothing a different color. But there was a disturbing proportion of cripples, higher than I recall seeing anywhere else, with stunted, twisted legs, many of them victims of polio, dragging themselves along, sometimes begging, sometimes just sitting in the dirt. Only a few were on crutches. And in the week we were in Dakar, we saw only one in a wheelchair.

The streets were lined with outdoor stalls, selling everything from hubcaps to chewing gum. The proprietors of the stalls sat, waiting for customers. Women sat on the ground, shelling groundnuts into baskets or sorting them into small plastic bags. Itinerant peddlers, mostly young men and boys, carried single items to sell: brooms; flashlight batteries, and one, whom we saw on several different days, unexpectedly and apparently unsuccessfully, an ironing board. Labor is not just cheap, it has essentially no cost at all. People were glad if they made the equivalent of a single dollar a day.

Not all Senegalese are so patient. Guidebooks and the U.S. State Department's tourist advisories warn against hustlers, pickpockets, snatch and grab thefts, and even in one area of expensive hotels along the Corniche of knifepoint muggings. Twice men started conversations while walking beside us and claimed, when they discovered we spoke English, that they had relatives in America and tried to detain us in what might have been the start of setups. We kept moving and did not ever really feel threatened or unsafe. Still we were not on the streets at night, wore cheap watches, and carried only small amounts of money.

The anchorage off the yacht club was completely safe. Presumably someone there had connections with local authorities who put out the word to leave the boats alone.

In a reversal of normal practice, the space left by the stalls on what would be sidewalks was taken up by parked cars, which forced pedestrians to walk in the streets, which were also filled with cars, trucks, and decrepit taxis. And, of course, goats.

Still, somehow, it all worked, and in Dakar we found the third world in some ways to be more efficient than the first. One of our main reasons to stop was to obtain Brazilian visas. We had tried to do this while in Gibraltar, but the Brazilian consulate in southern Portugal was never open and their embassy in Madrid informed us that it would take four weeks to process our applications. After clearing with the Senegalese authorities, which involved only one office and no baksheesh, we located the Brazilian Embassy and had our visas in hand two days later. Partially this may be because in late November ours were only the third and fourth visas issued to Americans by that Embassy in 2001.

Other ways in which the city proved efficient were Internet connections, easy to find, usually unutilized and costing about $1 per hour, and a supermarket where we discovered some useful products, such as Soft Scrub, that we never expected to see outside the U.S.

Downtown Dakar is centered on the Place de l'Indépendance, an open rectangle with some brownish grass amidst which are scattered sculptures and statues. Stained high-rise office buildings and hotels surround the square. We often ate lunch at one of them, the Hotel Indépendance, which was a good destination to give to the taxi drivers waiting outside the yacht club four miles away in suburban Hann. The hotel had a surprisingly good Chinese restaurant on a lower floor, and another restaurant on the eleventh floor, which also served food beside the unused rooftop swimming pool. This was an excellent spot, high above the teeming streets, from which to orient oneself in the city of more than one million inhabitants.

Streets run out from the Place de l'Indépendance in all directions. We took only two or three: one to a nearby open market where Carol, inspired by the colorful combinations of local costume, bought fabric for a couple of dollars a yard; another toward the post office, supermarket, port authority and our favorite Internet connection; and a third the few blocks down to the commercial docks, where we caught the ferry boat to the small island of Gorée a few miles out in the harbor.

Gorée is famous as a shipping point in the slave trade and is now described in guidebooks as an oasis of tranquility because it has no motor vehicles or even bicycles. It does have goats.

Gorée's importance in the slave trade is open to dispute. Certainly West Africa was the source of most of the slaves who were transported to the New World, but most came from areas further south and east. The village from which Alex Haley's ancestor was taken may have been in Gambia, a country a day's sail south of Dakar and completely surrounded by southern Senegal. Although we did not know it until we arrived in Brazil, we sailed the major slave route when we sailed to Salvador, Brazil, which was the landing place for half of all slaves taken to the Americas.

On Gorée there is a building named the Slave House, with an open portal onto the sea through which slaves were moved onto ships. There are old forts, a tiny harbor, several restaurants, and a lot of people trying to sell you something, particularly on the ferry ride, where tourists are captive audiences.

Regardless of the accuracy of historical details, Gorée is an apt place to consider the slave trade. One Senegalese, who was trying to sell us his services as a guide, offered the information that there are no longer any sharks around Gorée because there are no longer any slaves being thrown from ships. He said this as a joke. We found it disturbing on many levels, among them that he thought we would find this amusing.

The French tourists we saw on the ferryboats and on Gorée mostly stay in hotels on the north side of the peninsula, and I assume spend most of their time on the beaches there.

We spent most of our time in central Dakar or near the yacht club in Hann.

"Yacht club" is misleading. There are two clubs side by side on the beach in Hann, both vestiges of French colonial days, which ended forty years ago. Both appear to have been declining ever since. An unexpected number of boats are anchored off the clubs, mostly off the Cercle de la Voile de Dakar (CVD). We counted between fifty and sixty, about twenty of which were visitors. Of the local boats, at least half are semi-derelict, and few local club members are ever present. Nevertheless the clubs offer real services and are very good stops. We learned there that the masts we had seen in the cove on our way in were yet another rally, this one French and headed as we were for Salvador, Brazil.

The Cercle de la Voile de Dakar has sprawling grounds, with huge trees around a compound of whitewashed buildings, which include a bar, showers, a kitchen, and various other buildings. Many Senegalese seemed to live and work on the grounds. Outboard motors were always being repaired and laundry done. We had ours done, mostly what we call passage clothes, and because all laundry is routinely ironed in Dakar to kill eggs laid by a flying insect that can burrow into the skin when hatched, our passage clothes were for a while much nicer than our shore clothes.

Dakar is on the edge of the Sahara Desert and solidly in the region of northeast trade winds, which blew hard through the anchorage almost all the time we were there. Fine sand was carried back from the shore on clothes and shoes and blown by the wind.

A few hundred yards along the beach is an enormous open-air fish market.

We had passed many local fishing boats as we sailed into Dakar, and they were around us from dawn to dusk every day. The undecked pirogues range from small one-man craft, little more than dugout canoes, to boats twice the length of THE HAWKE OF TUONELA worked by a crew of more than twenty. All use the same method of laying out a net in a circle and pulling it in by hand. The bigger the boat, the bigger the net.

One Sunday we experienced within a few hundred yards the extremes of Senegalese social life. We ate lunch at a restaurant called La Corvette—after the class of small warships, not the American automobile—and then walked to the fish market, where the pirogues are pulled ashore or anchor just off, and the fishermen carry their fish through the water to makeshift stalls on the sand, where they are displayed on blocks of ice or in buckets of crushed ice. The variety of fish, the confusion, the dirt, the smells were stunning.

On the way back to the yacht club, walking on a street that showed occasional suggestions of broken pavement buried beneath Sahara sand, we passed the Equestrian Club, where there was a show jumping competition. We stopped and watched over the fence with some black children, then when we became tired standing, decided to go to the entrance and see if we could be admitted. The black man at the gate did so smilingly. There was no charge, but I doubt he would have admitted the children, although a majority of the audience sitting in the small grandstand was black, as were the competitors.

Senegal is a Muslim country, and after September 11 I reconsidered going there. The man I knew who had been to Dakar told me he did not think there would be a problem. Many of the Senegalese still wear beads to ward off the evil spirits of their former animist religion.

In foreign waters it is standard practice to fly your national flag from the stern of your vessel and a smaller courtesy flag of the country you are visiting from the lower starboard spreader near the mast.

Being in Dakar during the height of the action in Afghanistan I wondered about flying the flag, not wanting to become the target of a local radical. In the end I decided that discretion can too easily become pusillanimity and flew the flag. We were the only American boat in Dakar and were told by a local that we were the first in a long time. The overwhelming majority of visiting vessels are French. The only consequence of flying the American flag was an inaccurate comment from a British sailor who said we were brave.

We did hear of one sailor who was berated by a taxi driver when, not having local currency at his arrival, he paid his fare with U.S. dollars. The unfortunate sailor was Dutch. For just such a contingency we had obtained French francs in Gibraltar, and had no problem paying for lunch at La Corvette on the day we arrived, which was a Sunday, and receiving enough change in local currency to pay for our first taxi ride into the city and a bank the next day.

From the boat we heard the muezzin call the faithful to prayer at dawn and dusk and, on those occasions when we were on board, three more times during the day.

We lived an old movie cliché: Night. A boat anchored off the African coast. Suddenly the stillness is shattered by drums and singing chants. As far as we could tell the sounds came from the area that by day had been the fish market.

Less English is spoken in Dakar than other places we have been, but we heard disjointed pieces of a tragedy at the yacht club. One of the boats was a French catamaran with a distinctive paint job that we had seen several months earlier in Portimão, Portugal. The catamaran was owned and crewed by a husband and wife. Not far from the Canary Islands in full daylight and moderate weather the husband went forward to the mast to adjust a halyard, slipped and fell overboard. The wife saw him fall, but by the time she went below to get the key to start the engines and turned the boat, he was lost from view. She searched for him and ultimately sent out a distress call and others aided the search, but he was not found.

Some friends had helped her get the boat to Dakar. We did not know why she had come there, but did see her from time to time, a young woman devastated by grief.

When people first think about sailing oceans they fear statistical unlikely events such as survival storms or being hit by whales or freak waves. The real dangers are more mundane.

When we visited the port captain's office to clear for departure, the official solemnly examined the papers we had completed on arrival, asked a few questions in French about our next port, stamped the papers and handed them to me. In my broken French, I asked if he spoke English, he shook his head no, so I continued to say in French, "We like Senegal." He broke into a big smile and said, in English. "You come back."

15 Equator

I think of the Atlantic as being 3,000 miles wide, but between the bulges of Africa and Brazil it is only half that.

On the passage from Gibraltar to Dakar, I studied the charts repeatedly and considered options. We could save thousands of miles by continuing to follow the African coast or by heading south to St. Helena, then either directly to Cape Town or stopping first in Namibia, a country I had visited in RESURGAM and would very much like to see again.

Ignoring the realities of the wind it looked good, but as the Portuguese explorers discovered it is all wrong. Following the coast we would find a huge area of little to no wind where the continent turns due east for a thousand miles, and then when it turns south again we would be fighting the Benguela current and headwinds. The Portuguese must have been bitterly disappointed when the shore they had been following east for so long blocked them. They must have grown increasingly certain day by sweltering day that they had already rounded the last cape and were on their way to India.

Going via St. Helena, which I had also visited in RESURGAM coming from the other direction, would mean beating all the way from the Equator to Cape Town.

The longer way via Brazil should keep the wind behind the beam, and one of the lessons of my voyages is that a gale behind you is better than twenty knots on the nose. Besides I wanted to see more of Brazil than I had a decade earlier when Jill's illness limited us to Rio de Janeiro.

The wind obliged by doing what the pilot charts and the Coriolis Effect say it is supposed to do and gave us an uneventful ride to Salvador, Brazil, including some of the best sailing THE HAWKE OF TUONELA had yet known during a thousand-mile week reaching across the southeast trades.

As we approached the Equator I could not remember how many times I had crossed the line. A few minutes and a piece of paper to reconstruct past voyages led to the conclusion that this would be my eleventh crossing: four in EGREGIOUS; two in CHIDIOCK TICHBORNE; four in RESURGAM. The first and possibly the only for THE HAWKE OF TUONELA. Seven took place in the Pacific; one on the approaches to Singapore in the South China Sea; and this would make three in the Atlantic.

Except for the first two when EGREGIOUS sustained damage while heading from San Diego for Cape Horn, the crossings melded together in my memory.

Even in CHIDIOCK TICHBORNE, which was hardly the best light air performer, I was not stopped by the doldrums. I have come to believe that concern about them, like a lot of sailing lore, is a product of the days of slow sailing ships that did not go to windward and usually had foul bottoms.

Usually I have experienced a few unsettled days between the opposing circles of hemispheric winds—clockwise in the north; counterclockwise in the south—but often, as this year, there were only a few hours of wind moving toward the bow, requiring frequent sheet tightening. I recalled once in the Pacific on the way from Tahiti to San Diego going on deck after dark to make the hourly adjustment and being startled by torpedoes of phosphorescence flashing toward EGREGIOUS as dolphins sped through inky water seemingly to welcome us back north.

This year Carol and I had one slow afternoon. Even under spinnaker we oozed along at a couple of knots and I gave serious thought to dropping the sail and going overboard for my long intended cleaning of the prop and bottom of the bumper crop of gooseneck barnacles that had somehow managed to stow away. The water at the anchorage in Dakar was too dirty for me to go in there. A leftover swell caused me to decide to wait until the sea smoothed and we came to a complete stop. But we didn't. Near sunset the wind increased to six knots and backed toward the east. Carol kept asking if that was it, if these were the south-east trades; and after two days when we were only a degree north of the Equator, I finally said that I thought so.

I don't know why, perhaps it has something to do with the greater proportion of land in the northern hemisphere, but I have always found the transition between the trades to take place north of the Equator.

If I have neglected to mention that I have never powered through the doldrums, that is because it has never occurred to me to do so. EGREGIOUS and CHIDIOCK TICHBORNE were engineless; and on RESURGAM and THE HAWKE OF TUONELA, I generally power on ocean passages only to charge batteries or reach port before dark. Two or three hours, yes; two or three days, out of the question. If completely becalmed I go swimming.

I tried to reach back more than a quarter century across time to the man I was on those first two crossings; but I couldn't really. I had known how to sail and owned and lived on boats for half a dozen years along the California coast, but the open ocean was new and fresh for me. Both years I got hammered on the Equator, with thirty knots on the nose and short, vicious seas. I remembered wondering if this was what the SE trades were really like; if so I had been suffering from a serious delusion.

Just after I entered the southern hemisphere for the first time, those seas sheered off two ⅜-inch bolts which, in what seems to have been a design flaw, were intended to serve in lieu of tie-rods, and the mast began to leap about, soon breaking one of the lower tangs and forcing me to turn downwind and limp to Tahiti for repairs.

Next year those same seas cracked EGREGIOUS' fiberglass hull, but I had had enough of turning away from Cape Horn and kept on going, sailing and bailing, south and east for another four months and 18,000 miles.

Of course in the 1970s, navigating by sextant, I did not know precisely when I crossed the line. Now on a sunny, perfect morning, close reaching at seven knots under reefed main and partially furled jib—we could have carried full sail, but no longer in the business of setting records, I try to keep THE HAWKE OF TUONELA heeled less than 15°. We make passages just about as quickly, and I have often found that as the ride smoothes out, we actually go faster; and unquestionably life aboard is more comfortable—I turned on the chartplotter for the countdown. At 9:30 a.m. we were at 0°01.878′N.

Carol and I huddled around the chart table watching the numbers run down as if observing some religious rite. A few minutes later I said, "A mile to go," which, because we were not heading due south, was not strictly true.

At 9:46 the display momentarily showed all zeros, then started counting upward followed by an S. We had sailed from fall to spring. Once in the Pacific in RESURGAM I had three seasons in two days when I crossed the line on the last day of fall in the north into the last of spring followed by the first of summer in the south.

We went up on deck and looked astern. Of course there was no sign of the arbitrary divider, but I felt a lifting of spirit, a flush of pleasure, because I have a favorite hemisphere.

Once I made this comment to a couple at a party in Boston, but most people in the northern hemisphere are geographically challenged and they said quizzically, "The East?" The world is the United States and Europe and, maybe, Japan.

Although I did not enter it until the fourth decade of my life, I have sailed much more in the southern hemisphere than in the northern. The south has my favorite cities: Cape Town and Sydney; the cities with the most beautiful settings: Cape Town and Rio de Janeiro. To my eye the most beautiful islands: Lord Howe, Moorea; Bora-Bora; Bali. The greatest capes: Horn and Good Hope. And, for me, the best sailing in the SE Trades, which after those first two attempts at intimidation have proven as pleasant as I had expected, and in the westerlies of the Southern Ocean.

I looked south and felt it all opening out before me.

A symphony of blue and white.
Blue sky dotted with small regular puffs of cloud. Blue sea

speckled with white foam and THE HAWKE OF TUONELA's bow wave and wake. White sails arching up. A reef in the main; most of the jib set.

I sit in a Sport-a-seat on the port quarter in shorts and a T-shirt; from the cockpit speakers come the sounds of Marcelo Kayath playing Villa-Lobos and Piazzolla on the guitar. THE HAWKE OF TUONELA sings to the Brazilian and Argentinean accompaniment. Her bow carves a slice from one of the five-foot waves, and water runs back along her almost flush deck toward me. The day is warm and I don't mind getting wet. My eyes move from the instruments, which always read between 7 and 8 knots, to the sails, to the sky, to the ocean ahead. Everything is balanced. Everything is perfect. Everything is in tune. Well, almost everything.

The CD ends and I go below to change to a new disc. I open one of the three 100 disc storage albums. The sounds of the boat and the wind preclude my playing much classical music whose greater range is often lost. I choose a disc by a Spanish group, Gypsyland.

I glance at the port settee birth. Carol is sleeping. All I can see is one elegant bare leg draped over her lee cloth. If she is not exactly seasick, she is not exactly seawell either. Only one of us is in his element out here. There is nothing more I can do for her. I push the disc into the player and go back up on deck.

16 *Paradise With Cyberserpent*

In 1992 I missed one of the great cruising grounds in the world by sixty miles, perhaps even less, as RESURGAM approached the Brazilian coast from Montevideo, Uruguay. An acquaintance who had lived in Brazil had told me about Baia da Ilha Grande. I had studied the area on charts. But medical problems kept us in Rio de Janeiro for two months and we never made the single day sail west before having to move on. That is one of the reasons to keep sailing: the world changes; the sailor changes; and even familiar places can provide very different experiences on subsequent voyages.

This time Carol and I were coming from the opposite direction, the northeast.

Sometimes you get what you expect. Everyone knows that Brazilians are a sexy, musical people. Samba music blared out from the shore as we entered Baia de Todos os Santos and closed with the breakwater at Bahia Marina. Tropical flowers cascaded down lush, green hillsides. People sang and danced in the streets. It was a Hollywood musical, and it was also a few days before Christmas.

To the extent that any cultural generalization is valid, Brazilians are musical. Everywhere in the country, we found people singing, playing drums and guitars, in the streets, on ferry boats, at a table on a beach restaurant in the early evening darkness, usually not for money but simply to entertain themselves and their friends.

Salvador is a city of more than two million people. From seaward it looks like Miami Beach with hills. Near the harbor the old part of the city dates from the 1500s and includes what is reputed to be the world's largest collection of Baroque buildings.

Someone in Salvador wants the place to do business with yachts. The port actively solicits visitors. Several world races and rallies stop there. A French fleet made this our third successive port—the others being Dakar and Gibraltar—that we shared with rallies, and the fourth in less than six months. Visiting sailors have two choices. Most go to Centro Nautico in the heart of the city; we stayed at the newer, quieter, beautifully landscaped Bahia Marina, a half-mile away.

Salvador is built on two levels. The central business district and government offices are on a narrow coastal strip, while the old Baroque buildings and most of the shopping is on hilltops more than a hundred feet higher, reached by a public elevator that carries tens of thousands of people a day, or very steep streets.

Along that coastal strip I had my first really bad day since leaving Boston. While we were trying to locate four different Brazilian government offices to clear into the country in 95°F heat, something I had eaten ate back. It took two days and a lot of misdirected footsteps to find all the officials in all the offices in the required sequence. The officials, when found, were pleasant, and the only unusual aspect of the clearance was the particular attention the health inspector paid to our water supply. How much did we have aboard? Where had we taken it on? How did we purify? Cholera has been endemic along the Amazon for years and Brazilians do not want it to travel south.

Having overcome Brazilian bureaucracy and my internal bug and having located the necessities of life, including a shopping mall with a supermarket and an Internet connection, we settled in to renew an acquaintance with caipirinhas—a Brazilian mixed drink made with cane alcohol and lime juice; await postal mail for the first time in several months; and enjoy the tropical, holiday atmosphere.

Although a third of the country, roughly 60,000,000 people, lives on less than $40 a month, there are still enough shoppers to make the malls as crowded as in the U.S. Santa Claus wears the same red suit with white trim and has the same long white beard in Brazil as he does in the U.S., but in Brazil in December he sweats more.

Christmas Day was hot and quiet. We stayed on the boat until midafternoon when I suggested we take a walk to see if any restaurants were open. The lower part of the city was deserted, but when we rode the elevator to the upper level, we stepped into one of those serendipitous experiences that are an unpredictable pleasure of wandering the world.

On an earlier visit to the upper city, we had turned right when we left the elevator, walked around, saw a few buildings of minor interest, and wondered what the fuss was about. This time we turned left, and that, as Robert Frost has observed, made all the difference. Down a couple of blocks and around a corner, we found the true old heart of the city, with narrow cobblestoned walkways, what would be called sidewalk cafes except that they are in the middle of the streets, incredibly ornate Baroque churches, Christmas decorations, and Salvadorians. Having spent the day at home, families were now emerging to celebrate the holiday publicly. Over caipirinhas at a sidewalk table and later dinner in a nearby restaurant, we watched the promenade, and on our way back to the boat just after dark, stopped to listen to a choir of middle aged women dressed in nurses' uniforms sing Christmas carols in Portuguese. This was a Christmas to remember.

Into this paradise, the serpent came, appropriately for a new millennium, by e-mail. Cyberserpent. In the form of an offer for Carol to rejoin her former firm as a principal. This required discussion, which required setting up a conference call. Call completed; our mail arrived; Carol's decision unmade; we left the marina to spend a few days at the north end of the bay.

Baia de Todos os Santos is twenty miles deep and ten miles wide. Part of the bay is shallow, but a dozen islands and two rivers offer more anchorages than we had time for. In fact we never got beyond the first that had been recommended to us by a local sailor, an isolated cove between Ilha dos Frades, Ilha do Bom Jesus, and the mainland.

Moving a half-mile past a small village on Bom Jesus, we anchored near the head of the cove, surrounded by hillsides covered with unbroken jungle and silence broken only by birdcalls.

During the four days we stayed there, a few other boats came in and out, mostly French ralliers, but they anchored closer to the village, and we swam in the warm water, read, watched a few local fishermen working near the shore in dug out canoes, and considered ships and sealing wax and architectural careers and kings.

Twice we rowed to the village, where the advantages of oars, in addition to exercise, were once again proven, when we picked up our Avon Redstart and carried it across the shallow flats, while the French struggled with their outboard laden dinghies. We even had the satisfaction of giving a Frenchman a ride out to his dinghy, which he had left tied to a pole in what the incoming tide turned into chest deep water.

While the fishermen of Bom Jesus are poor, the village is not because most of the men work at an oil refinery on the nearby mainland. There is not much in the way of provisions in the few small dark shops; water is drawn from a community well; but most of the houses are neat and well kept, and brilliant red flamboyant trees frame a small white church near a short jetty.

When we went ashore on December 30 the village was busy. Muddy young men were joyously playing soccer on the flats exposed by the outgoing tide; stalls were selling drinks in the church square; and we watched a man pole a dug out canoe up to the jetty, conveying a huge, live pig to a waiting launch which would take it to another village to be consumed in a New Year's feast.

Under cloudy skies we sailed for Rio de Janeiro on New Year's Eve, covering most of the 700 miles in three days before the skies cleared, the sun shown, and the wind disappeared.

That night the sky to the south was ablaze—literally not poetically—with flames from platforms of a huge offshore oil field.

In the morning as we ghosted south, workboats and helicopters busily conveyed workers between the twenty mile distant mainland and the platforms, and the next night a fleet of small fishing boats crowded the ocean, so we powered for a few hours to gain elbow room.

My principle about not entering ports at night was compromised by the return of strong following wind off Cape Frio, where the Brazilian coast makes a sharp turn to the west sixty miles east of Rio de Janeiro. There being no way I could slow us down sufficiently to wait until dawn, I let THE HAWKE OF TUONELA romp on at eight knots, which brought the mouth of Guanabara Bay into view just at nightfall. The harbor is huge, getting into it is hardly threading a needle, but I worry about what I can't see, and even in daylight ten years earlier I found the place full of debris, including plastic bags, one of which wrapped about RESURGAM's propeller. The prospect of a night dive was not appealing. Neither was spending twelve hours sailing on and off the coast in strong wind. So after examining the chart, which shows many underwater cables and areas where anchoring is prohibited, I put a safe waypoint in the GPS and we powered slowly in.

Sugarloaf was a huge dark shape looming sinisterly above us to port; beyond it were strings of lights of Copacabana and Ipanema. To starboard was an area of darkness around an old fort.

Inside the headlands too many lights became visible, including several from aircraft landing at Rio's domestic airport which we momentarily mistook for ships' running lights, and some puzzling shapes which seemed to be on a collision course with us until we realized that they were the illuminated supports of a distant bridge.

Just after 10:00 p.m. I let the anchor go a few yards from our safe waypoint off Niterói on the east side of the harbor.

"Well, how do you like Rio?" I asked Carol.

"I'll let you know in the morning."

Morning revealed a cove that would by itself be a fine harbor with a couple of marinas, one of which belongs to the Brazilian Navy and, as we later learned, welcomes visiting yachts.

After breakfast we powered the four miles across to the more

Copacabana and Ipanema Beaches, Rio de Janeiro

conveniently located Marina da Gloria, and Carol saw how beautiful Rio is. The place is other worldly, a landscape from a science fiction fantasy, with impossible mountains turned onto their sides and stuck into the shore beside wide white beaches. It is easy to understand why the Portuguese who stumbled upon Brazil five hundred years ago seriously wondered if they had discovered the Garden of Eden.

We spent two weeks in Rio and did all the usual tourist things. We ate a great many gelatos—small barbecued chickens; had feijoada at the incongruously named Maxim's Restaurant at Copacabana; lunch at the outdoor tables at the foot of the Christ statue on Corcovado; and enjoyed sunsets from HAWKE's cockpit, watching cranes hunt and fish leap in the harbor.

Although it sometimes seems that half of Brazil's population is being paid to watch the other half and locals warned us about street crime, I found the harbor and the city to be cleaner and safer than I had on my first visit. One Brazilian told us, "Back then we called Marina da Gloria, Latrina da Gloria." While another explained, "We have a bad government now; but the last one was worse."

We had a wonderful time, so good in fact that Carol decided to return after seeing South Africa to what most people consider to be the real world, but some of us know is only one of many.

Later we were asked to write about that decision, and those words probably cannot be improved upon.

Carol

Freedom, adventure, discovery, the appeals and the reality of cruising life. A dream compared to the daily routine and demands of land life, a job, and all the obligations that come with it. But what if your cruising plans were open ended and you never knew when or if you were going back home? Would you feel cut adrift or blissfully content to take life one hour, one day at a time without care for the future beyond the next port of call?

Webb and I left Boston in May 2001 to sail indefinitely. I eagerly looked forward to my second Atlantic crossing and possibly my first circumnavigation. The two-year plan was for Webb to complete his fourth circumnavigation in Australia and then continue on into the South Pacific. Our plans beyond were open ended. To face the challenges of the ocean and explore the world, I left an architectural career and life behind that were twenty years in the making. After 12,000 miles of blue water passages and unforgettable landfalls in the Azores, Portugal, Spain, Gibraltar, West Africa, Brazil and South Africa, the feeling of being cut adrift has not abated for me.

Almost 100 days of our first year were spent on passages. I felt the most disconnected from life then. There is a kind of sensory deprivation that occurs on a small boat at sea. It happens very quickly as you move offshore loosing sight of land and all signs of its inhabitants. You are left with a few constant and unrelenting sensations, the sound of water rushing past the hull, the movement of the boat pounding to windward, rolling downwind, or bouncing gently on a beam reach, and the day/night cycle. This routine is broken by the occasional dolphin show, passing ship, wind shift, and mechanical breakages. Food is either dried or canned and its consumption a chore rather than a pleasure. Sleep is rarely uninterrupted by standing watch or sudden changes in the boat's motion. Reading, occasional conversation and memories become the only links to the life left behind. Catching first sight and smell of land at the end of a passage makes one realize just how isolated life at sea had become.

At sea Webb reconnects with one of the essentials of his life. He wrote that the "rubber band" effect that Boston held over him for seven years was finally broken when we cast off dock lines for the last time. His connections to the world are through sailing, writing and wife. For him all three are portable connections. My sense of connection to the world is through career, friends, family, home, and husband. Of these only the husband seems to be portable.

Now a year later the Boston "rubber band" is pulling me back. When the offer came for me to return to my former architectural firm as a principal the time seemed right for me to reconnect. Webb will continue his fourth circumnavigation. I will become an avid part-time cruiser, spending six weeks a year with Webb on THE HAWKE OF TUONELA wherever they may be. And just maybe the Boston "rubber band" will snatch Webb up from time to time, conveyed by airline if not sailboat. I will enjoy fixed land connections, Webb his portable ocean connections. Hopefully our connection to each other will bring us the best of both worlds.

Webb

Sailing is not essential to most people, probably not even to most people who own boats. It is just one of the things they do in the summer, as they go skiing in winter, and play tennis or golf whenever. Sailing is essential for me; it is not for Carol. Her identity is not as a sailor, but as an architect. In her career she is a round peg in a round hole, and the only surprising thing is that she ever thought she wanted a different kind of life.

Transitions are always hard. Over the past thirty years I have observed many couples out cruising for the first time, and they seem to share two common problems: excessive propinquity and exposure to what they perceive because of inexperience as danger at sea.

Carol and I had to deal with the first, though not the second. We were not in danger between Boston and Cape Town—and did not ever mistakenly think we were—only sometimes uncomfortable.

Ironically we had successfully completed the transition from land to sea life and were having a wonderful Christmas when the exploratory e-mail from Carol's former firm reached her in Salvador, Brazil. Perhaps that was best, so that there was no question about needing to give sailing more time. And although she gave the matter thought for several weeks and did not formally accept the offer until we had sailed on to Rio de Janeiro, I never had any doubt about what her decision would be.

My only contributions to that decision were to affirm that it was hers alone, that she should make it solely on the basis of what would make her happier, and that I personally was not going to live again in Boston full time unless compelled to do so by decrepitude.

Carol has given her reasons. A friend asked if it would have mattered if we had been at sea less, and she replied that it would not, she liked the change of scene, if not the passages themselves, and would have become bored had we stayed longer in one place.

For me, as for Carol, the decision is both negative and positive. The United States is not home for me as it is for Carol. THE HAWKE OF TUONELA is my home. And now I will be drawn back there to possessions and complications I had chosen to sail away from. Beyond that I enjoyed our being together. Although 7/24/365 is too much and we need some time apart, we both think our new arrangements probably has the desirable ratio almost exactly reversed.

For me one of the positives is the sailing. I have mostly sailed alone, and I am looking forward to returning to the solitude of the sea, to an uncompromised purity of experience. Carol seldom complained, but it could not be concealed during a passage that someone aboard the boat was wishing only that it would be over.

So we have that newest of relationships: an e-marriage.

Yet it is not really new at all. New England sailors and their wives have long lived apart. Instead of sailing off for a year to China or four years whaling, I will fly back at shorter intervals. Carol will just have to have the widow's walk installed at her Charlestown condominium facing Logan airport instead of the harbor.

As the French writer Alphonse Karr observed, "The more things change, the more they stay the same."

Carol's decision made, we sailed, or rather powered out of Rio de Janeiro in a spectacular Turner-painted dawn toward the long anticipated Ilha Grande—pronounced in Brazilian as though the 'd' is 'g'—fifty-five miles west.

At sunset a fleet of colorfully painted daytrip schooners was powering out of Enseada das Palmas, the first reachable anchorage near the east end of the island, to return to their home base at Abraao, as we powered in and dropped anchor a hundred yards off a narrow ribbon of white sand in 25 feet of dark green water. Beyond the sand two or three small houses poked roofs through thick foliage and off to one side stood a handful of bungalows belonging to a backpacker hostel frequented by surfers.

During the long years in Boston, what I remembered most fondly of sailing was actually being at sea and at quiet anchorages. When we left I knew that our route would keep us mostly in cities and marinas for the first year. Enseada das Palmas was serene introduction to forty miles of cruising paradise, reminiscent both of New Zealand's Bay of Islands and the French Marquesas Islands in the South Pacific.

The next morning, while drinking coffee in the cockpit as the sun climbed over the hills and filled the bay with light, we observed the beginning of the cove's daily routine, when boys began sleepily setting out plastic tables and chairs at two beachside restaurants and the first surfers emerged from the hostel carrying their boards and disappeared into the jungle up a steep trail leading to the seaward side of the island. About 11:00 daytrip boats began to arrive: some going alongside a small pier to discharge their passengers, others simply heading in until their bows were on the beach and letting the day trippers jump into the warm water. By noon the shoreline was full of boats held by bow lines tied to palm trees and makeshift stern anchors. A steady procession huffed up the trail over the pass to the ocean beach. The tables were full. In late afternoon the procession returned; the tables emptied. People climbed, were lifted, or unceremoniously if good naturedly pushed up to the decks of schooners. Boys restacked tables and chairs. The shore was deserted except for a dog romping along, chasing birds that we saw everywhere in Brazil that looked very much like vultures, but perhaps were not. And by sunset we and the crews of one or two Brazilian yachts once again had the cove to ourselves.

Paradise with day-trippers? Somehow they did not spoil the place, except for Easter weekend when the entire island was as jammed as an American park on the Fourth of July; and when we wanted complete solitude, there were plenty of other coves.

One afternoon we followed the procession up the steep narrow trail overhung with thick vegetation, where we saw a family of marmoset peering down in hope of a handout, over the ridge and descended to what belongs on any list of the ten best beaches in the world.

A mile long crescent of white sand is bound by a tree covered point at one end and a jumble of boulders at the other. Blue water with three or four lines of good waves. And all pristine.

Not a single permanent sign of man. Not a building, not a food stall, and, of course, not a road. There are none on Ilha Grande, and the only motorized vehicle we saw on the island belonged to the police in Abraao, presumably as a symbol of prestige for they can't drive it more than a few hundred yards. All those people we had seen climbing up the trail were really very few and occupied only a small portion of the sand.

Although I spent a lot of time on beaches as a boy, since buying my first boat almost four decades ago, I have not. The last thing my skin needs is more sun, so we found a shady spot beneath the trees at the edge of the sand. One could not help but notice that there are a great many attractive young people on Ilha Grande. The girl from Ipanema's more beautiful sister vacations there.

After a while we joined the youth in the water, and I body surfed for the first time since Bali more than a decade earlier. My third wave was perfect, a wild, exhilarating ride that carried me past Carol all the way to the beach. The first wave of my 60s, and, briefly, I was a teenager again. Briefly is long enough.

village of Abraao, Ilha Grande, Brazil. One of the last great unspoiled
grounds

On other afternoons we rowed ashore and tied the painter to a palm tree a few steps from one of the plastic tables, where we sat and drank cold beers or caipirinhas and ate heaping plates of grilled shrimp. The total bill often came to as much as $5 or $6. Once a helicopter buzzed over from the mainland and three young men emerged, strolled over, had lunch, then flew away. That was an expensive plate of shrimp, I thought, before I considered that we had spent considerably more in getting there than they had.

I don't know if Enseada das Palmas was our favorite anchorage at Ilha Grande. I don't know how long we stayed there. After cruising to Parati, about forty miles west at the far end of Baia da Ilha Grande, we returned. I don't know how long we spent in the whole area. It was that kind of place.

Ilha Grande is sixteen miles long and six miles at its widest. Its green mountains rise to over 3,000 feet. The island parallels the mainland to the north, where a range of gray blue mountains rises quickly to over 5,000 feet. The tourist literature says there are 365 islands in the bay, one for every day of the year. And in addition to the islands there are coves and anchorages along the mainland.

When we moved from Enseada das Palmas, we discovered the two negatives of the area. The anchor and chain came up covered with black, viscous mud and required tedious cleaning; and, in summer, at least for us, there was little to no wind, which doesn't make too much difference when you are only going a few miles around a headland to the next cove.

There is more to the village of Abraao, which was in the next cove, than appears from the anchorage, where one sees only a few two story shops and restaurants. Paths that almost could be called streets lead to a maze of small hotels and campgrounds carved from the jungle; ferry boats run to Angra dos Reis, ten miles away on the mainland; the harbor is full of the daytrip mock schooners; and the Brazilian custom of self-serve buffet restaurants called comida a kilo, where you put whatever you want on your plate which is then weighed to determine what you pay, has taken a new and dangerous turn with ice cream a kilo.

Beyond Abraao is the almost completely enclosed Enseada da Estrella, by far the best protected of the anchorages, though there was no serious weather while we were in the area, and with one of the best restaurants, with moorings for those who need them.

From Estrella, we powered to Angra dos Reis, where we had been told there is a marina where it is convenient to take on supplies. The stores on Ilha Grande are minimally stocked, and there are no banks. Not even an ATM. Locals ride the ferry to shop in Angra. The marina proved to be the aptly named Marina Piratas. With an adjacent shopping center, the marina is indeed convenient. And charging $50 a night for a boat the size of THE HAWKE OF TUONELA, or three times more than we had paid in both Salvador and Rio de Janeiro, they are indeed pirates.

Fueled, watered, provisioned and with a fresh supply of cash, we made the great leap—all of twenty miles—to the grandeur of the Saco de Mamangua near the west end of the bay. Steep mountains with great exposed walls of rock rise from both sides of the fjord-like Saco. We anchored a mile inside the headlands, near a small rocky island, and a couple of hundred yards off one of the scattered vacation homes on the shoreline. We spent two peaceful days there before moving on to the old port of Parati.

More than a hundred years ago, Parati, located at the end of a railway track from inland gold mines, was one of the major ports of Brazil, and the source of the wealth the original pirates of Angra dos Reis preyed upon. Although it is on a world heritage list and has an area of old whitewashed buildings with prettily painted doorways, we found it touristy and less enjoyable than other places we had anchored, so we powered back east to the beauty, grilled shrimp, beaches and ice cream of Ilha Grande.

Although we usually shared anchorages with other cruising boats, none of the anchorages was overcrowded, except for E˞ ˺er weekend, and except for two French boats, presumably ˼ff from the rally in Salvador, and a handful flying the Ar- ˼n flag, all the boats were Brazilian. I can't think of any other cruising ground in the world this good that is this un-crowned, not to mention inexpensive.

If Baia da Ilha Grande is one version of paradise, as Adam and Eve and Carol know, even paradise can pale, and the desire to reach South Africa before the onset of the southern winter finally compelled us to sail east from Eden.

17 A Broken Wheel

The rim fell off the wheel of wind we expected to carry us to Cape Town. After eighteen hours of good sailing once we had powered to the ocean side of Ilha Grande, the wind died and we were becalmed.

It was a beautiful day. Warm, pleasant, high blue sky, smooth sea. A perfect day for the beach; but not for sailing. The first of many, far too many. So many that this passage was unique in that we began to long for bad weather, kept glancing at the barometer hoping to see it fall and herald an approaching front. We lolled around, read, listened to music. After all we were in no rush and there were only 3,300 miles to go.

The plan was to sail southeast until we reached the westerlies which would carry us to Africa. Our point of departure was 23°S. Our destination 33°S. I thought we might have to go down to 40°S to find west wind. It was a reasonable plan. But it did not happen. Not even close.

When toward evening on that first full day at sea, the wind did return, it blew all night at 25 knots from the southeast, and a swell from the south killed us on port tack. THE HAWKE OF TUONELA could make three knots south or six knots east. Naturally we went east, telling ourselves that we had plenty of time and distance to get south. Ah, the optimism of youth.

The flanker, a former racing sail I use as a cruising spinnaker, got more airtime during that beautiful month in the South Atlantic than it had in all its previous long and distinguished life. Often it was the only sail that would fill in the zephyrs, and too often there was a swell coming from lows somewhere far, way too far to the south, that collapsed it.

The culprit was the South Atlantic high, which had decided to wander south, and which slowly, inexorably drew us into its empty arms.

When we did eventually reach Cape Town, a South African sailor told me that once when he was returning from Brazil he had to go all the way to 50°S before he found the westerlies. I had no intention of taking Carol to 50°S on her last ocean passage. I had no desire to go there myself just then. And my desires were of course irrelevant anyway. THE HAWKE OF TUONELA had developed a mind of her own. Whenever I pointed her bow south, she merely tapped her fingers, rocking up and down in place; when I gave up and again reluctantly pointed her bow east, she usually condescended to sail slowly.

Fine day followed fine day and with few exceptions the passage was painless, if boring. Carol was scheduled to fly back to Boston from Cape Town in June and this was only February. I was confident we'd make it. Maybe even with a few days to spare. All we had to do was maintain a daily average of 33 miles and we'd be there by the end of May, and we were able to do that. At least most of the time.

The least exceptional of the exceptions to boredom came one afternoon near mid-ocean when while sitting on deck listening to music and watching an albatross fly a search pattern I noticed a patch of blue sky though a hole in the leech of the jib at the level of the lower spreader, whose chaffing gear had chaffed through. The sound of the sail being lowered brought Carol to the companionway.

Years ago a sailmaker taught me that the best way to repair sails at sea is to use contact cement. This after I had spent my first circumnavigation hand-stitching EGREGIOUS' sails, which were new for the voyage but made too lightly for the southern ocean. No American sailmaker then had any knowledge of what the southern ocean requires because no American sailor had tried to go there. When I reached Auckland after five months at sea in 1975-76, the main sail was Swiss cheese and completely unusable below the first reef. Contact cement is easier, faster and stronger.

While the patch was drying, Carol hauled me up the mast. The day was similar to the one when I went up the mast on the way to the Azores eight months earlier and 5,000 miles almost due north. Little wind, low rolling swell. Although I had to spend more time aloft this time, I didn't have to go all the way to the masthead and didn't get banged up as much.

After crisscrossing several rounds of self-amalgamating tape, which sometimes amalgamates and sometimes doesn't, over the spreader tip, I had Carol lower me to the deck. On my way down I noticed a broken strand of wire on the baby stay. Aloft again, this time with duct tape.

Before taking the bosun's chair below I studied the mast and all the rest of the rigging. Satisfied, I stowed the equipment, raised the jib, and went back to sleep until Africa.

Actually I didn't sleep quite all the rest of the way to Africa. It only seemed that way. One night a few hundred miles from Cape Town Carol and I were both rudely awakened by the sickening crack of breaking metal. In the dark it took me a while to determine that one of the two tie rods had snapped. This was probably the least critical piece of metal that could have broken. Atypically THE HAWKE OF TUONELA has tie rods both forward and aft of the mast, and the second one was enough to keep the deck from flexing.

The most exceptional of the exceptions was a worm that appeared in the headliner one morning followed by perhaps the most dangerous thirty seconds of the entire voyage.

A typical fine, sunny morning. THE HAWKE OF TUONELA sailing smoothly and slowly east. Carol and I on the settee berths in the main cabin reading. She on port, nearer the batteries and electrical panel. I to starboard. A minute earlier Carol had said, "I smell something funny. Like something burning."

"I don't smell anything," I said, but put my book down and looked around. First at the stove, then the engine box, though the engine was off, then the electrical panel. I stood and went to the companionway. Everything appeared normal.

I returned to my berth and sat down.

Carol repeated, "I still smell it."

As I leaned back, I saw the worm appear in the overhead. From its location I knew immediately that it was the wire from the deck mounted solar panel melting through the headliner. I leapt for the port quarter berth, pulled up the cushion and the plywood top of the battery compartment. Acrid smoke rose from blackening wires and the solar panel regulator. I reached in and ripped the wires away, burning myself slightly in the process. Carol had grabbed a fire extinguisher, but it was not needed. The danger was over. Still it was one of those "what if?" moments. What if we had been in the cockpit or napping? What if Carol hadn't caught the first whiff of smoldering plastic?

The culprit was a $15 metal through-deck connection for the solar panel wires that had short circuited. A fuse in the wiring system was obviously in the wrong place. Little damage was done; but the batteries are located directly in front of the diesel tank and surrounded by wood and plastic that would have burned in I don't know how long. Five minutes more? Ten? My imagination is too good. I could see the boat consumed by flames. But it didn't happen. And THE HAWKE OF TUONELA continued to sail gently on.

There is something to be said for boredom.

The high points of the passage were the lows. Twice the eternally high barometer quivered. How many times, I wondered, have I looked at a barometer during a storm and wanted to see it rise? Now pleased to see a millimeter fall I moved to the companionway and tried to will a band of clouds into existence.

In a few hours it worked and clouds materialized and moved toward us. Soon the shining blue sky had turned a splendid shade of gray. Sweet overcast. Delightful gloom. And best of all: wind.

Waves rose from the inert sea. Huge tumblers—comparatively—towering two and even three feet high. THE HAWKE OF TUONELA's bow wave began to begin. The boat speed indicator reached into forgotten realms of five and six knots.

A few more hours and the wind actually became decent, 20 to 25 knots, and our speed an unheard of seven to eight.

But both fronts moved too fast and were beyond us in less

than twenty-four hours. The wind died. The seas fell flat. And THE HAWKE OF TUONELA resumed inching her reluctant way east.

A month after Ilha Grande disappeared astern, the chartplotter claimed that land was just over the horizon ahead. We had been listening to Cape Town radio stations for several days, and now one of them gave us a storm warning along with the evening news. A fast moving front was approaching from the west, with near gale force winds and rough seas due along the coast. While this was not exactly what we wanted to hear, it was not too alarming. The approach to Cape Town is open and the harbor itself well protected by a double ring of breakwaters. I assumed—incorrectly as I later learned—that the harbor could be entered under any conditions, although I was concerned about maneuvering under power in strong winds in the relatively tight quarters of the Royal Cape Yacht Club docks.

There was no indication of any of this at that moment aboard THE HAWKE OF TUONELA. The barometer remained high and steady. The sky as clear and as blue as it had been almost uniformly for a month.

I would have slept lightly that night anyway, but with the forecast I slept even lighter.

At sunset we were sailing easily at four knots under full sail. The wind came up with the full moon. They rose together until by midnight THE HAWKE OF TUONELA under deeply furled jib was tearing through a silver and black world of magical beauty. I knew I needed to get another hour or two of sleep before the line of clouds which was spreading over the western sky reached us; but the power of the boat racing through such a scene kept me on deck. I could feel the boat, the motion, the force of the wind, each wave of an obsidian sea, deep inside, exhilarating.

3:00 a.m. saw the first of two sudden changes when the front reached us with a brief burst of forty-knot wind and pouring rain. I was pressed down into my bunk as we heeled far over. Carol behind her lee cloth called, "What's happening?"

Pulling myself upright, I replied, "The front has finally hit." I checked our heading on the cabin instrument readout. Predictably the wind had veered and we were heading north, almost 70° off course.

I didn't expect the onslaught to last long and let us run off for ten minutes until, when the rain eased and the wind dropped back into the twenties, I went on deck and jibed the scrap of jib and set the Monitor to steer us east again.

A foggy dawn saw the other change, an abrupt drop in ocean temperature from 70°F to 50°F, as we entered the cold north-flowing Benguela Current.

I had looked forward to seeing Table Mountain from the west. When I left Cape Town in 1988, I could still discern its shape sixty miles away. Now I could see land only on the radar, which somehow wasn't quite the same.

The fog and cold water chilled us for the first time since leaving Gibraltar and we dug out Polartec to wear under our foul-weather gear. Small penguins bobbed in the waves and seals raised their heads curiously to watch the apparition that was THE HAWKE OF TUONELA pass.

Midmorning saw the fog burn off and the wind die. The first was good news; the second was not.

During the night we had moved from thousands of feet of water to hundreds and now as we closed the coast waves built and crested just as the stabilizing influence of the wind was lost. The Monitor could not handle the conditions and neither could the tiller pilot. Both can react only after a boat has gone off wind angle or compass course. Neither can see or feel waves or anticipate. I had to hand steer to keep THE HAWKE OF TUONELA from being too violently thrown around in the shelving sea.

The lull was brief, but by the time the wind returned we were only a few hundred yards off Green Point, beyond which is the outer breakwater of the port of Cape Town. We powered on, down the face of dangerously curling waves that had risen to 15 feet. I kept thinking that one of them would break. We and they were just on the verge. In a month of glassy seas I had envisioned powering easily across the approach to Cape Town, admiring the beauty of the landscape and the city. Now beauty was forgotten as I concentrated on our converging angle with the breakwater and the violently rolling waves. There are times when there simply is no margin for error, and almost always, maybe always, such times come close to land.

Teetering, bracing myself with my feet against a teak strip in the center of the cockpit sole, holding onto the tiller with both hands, hoping that the always reliable Yanmar didn't choose this moment to become temperamental, seeing Carol on the opposite side of the cockpit with her arms wrapped around a winch, until suddenly we were past the point and into the protection of the outer breakwater. The waves vanished. Safe. I felt the tension release my shoulders, flow from my entire body. Carol and I smiled a bit wanly at one another.

"I'm glad that's over," she said.

"So am I."

I meant the last stretch of rough water. Carol meant more.

PART III

ALONE AGAIN

18 *Alone Again, Unnaturally*

THE HAWKE OF TUONELA was heeled 5° to starboard, which wasn't bad for gale force winds that shook the boat and rattled normally secure halyards. It may have helped that we were in a cradle at the small boatyard at the Royal Cape Yacht Club and not at sea. Carol had flown back to Boston a month earlier, where she quickly bought a condo, a Volvo, a winter wardrobe and settled in. "We" now was THE HAWKE OF TUONELA and me.

I had always planned to spend the southern winter in South Africa, a country with which I have no connections other than that apparently we were all Africans to begin with, but for which I feel a strong affinity. Had Carol remained, we would have made our way in stages along the coast to Durban, reversing the course I had followed in RESURGAM in 1987-88; but once her decision was made I decided that if I could find a satisfactory spot for THE HAWKE OF TUONELA, I would keep her in Cape Town until it was time to sail for Australia. Traveling out of season—most visiting yachts cruise South Africa in the southern summer—there was no problem in obtaining a slip at the most hospitable Royal Cape Yacht Club. Being in Cape Town, which has as beautiful a setting as any city in the world, was hardly a sacrifice.

The haul out had been for routine antifouling, and like everything else in South Africa was inexpensive, particularly in 2002 when the exchange rate for the rand ballooned briefly from 7 to the US dollar to 14 and then settled for several months at about 11.

The exchange rate was one of the salient facts of life in Cape Town that year, as omnipresent as Table Mountain. An international bank paid what seemed to be a huge fine to the govern-

Cape Town: as beautiful a setting as any city in the world

ment without specifically admitting that they had manipulated the currency. The rumor was that they had made a billion dollars and paid back two hundred million, which isn't a bad two month return. I don't understand how you manipulate a currency, but an undoubted consequence was that South Africa which was among the most inexpensive countries to a western standard in the world at seven rand to the dollar was exceedingly, almost embarrassingly inexpensive at 10 to 11. I am not accustomed to being a rich foreigner. Things were so cheap we ended up spending far more than we had planned on bargains that just couldn't be passed up.

In the year that it had taken THE HAWKE OF TUONELA to carve a big Z across the North and South Atlantic Oceans from Boston to Cape Town, she had covered 12,000 miles and been underway for 130 days, of which 97 were spent on ocean passages. I have read that cruisers only sail one day in ten, so perhaps I am not a cruiser. Over the years I have found that, as I did in THE HAWKE OF TUONELA, I sail one day in three.

144

The breakdown of the passages was: Boston—Azores 17 days; Azores—Lisbon 7; Gibraltar—Dakar 15; Dakar—Salvador 18; Salvador—Rio de Janeiro 7; Brazil—Cape Town 33.

Disappointingly none of these was fast, and the last decidedly slow. To make good passages you need sustained reaching conditions, which thus far THE HAWKE OF TUONELA had found only on that final week to Salvador, Brazil, when she reached across the Southeast Trades to her only 1,000-mile week. In RESURGAM I had many 1,000-mile weeks and the slightly bigger HAWKE should be a half-knot faster. I expected that her time would come when we entered the Forties on the way to Australia.

Overall the old boat had held up well, but then not much other than the hull and deck was old. During the five years preceding our departure I had replaced practically everything from the rudder to the mast. However there had been inevitable wear. The port lower shroud needed to replaced, along with the babystay and the tie rod, and there were hairline cracks in the boom which was original equipment. At South African prices it was cheaper to have a new boom made than repair the old one, which also solved a problem of chaff on the outhaul.

I also was seduced into finally replacing my old Barient winches, which still worked perfectly but were not self-tailers, with new Andersen self-tailing winches. Although a Danish import, these were already in stock and cost half what they would have in the U.S.

I replaced the batteries and a cockpit speaker that is supposed to be waterproof, but isn't quite, and various wiring.

A sailmaker professionally redid the patch I had glued on the jib at sea.

There were other maintenance chores and repairs and improvements, mostly minor, which along with writing kept me occupied, but I missed Carol. Despite the wives and women, I have spent most of my life alone; but not for a while, and at least for a while being alone again in port did not come naturally.

19 *In the Shadow of Table Mountain*

Two days later we were back in the water and again on an even keel.

The relaunching went well, if not smoothly, and THE HAWKE OF TUONELA was afloat at 1:00 p.m. and in her slip a few minutes later.

The boatyard has an unusual method of moving boats about. Its concrete surface is broken into squares four or five yards—presumably meters—to a side with seams between them. Cradles are pulled on solid metal wheels by a steel cable that runs to a winch at one end of the yard. Direction is controlled by rearranging big pulleys attached to various padeyes in the concrete and realigning the wheels every few feet by pounding them with a sledgehammer. Creaking, groaning, lurching, clanging until the cradle is within reach of the crane. I sat on the sidelines and watched and told myself that they do this all the time and there isn't a pile of shattered hulls anywhere in sight.

All in all it was about as good a haul out as I can recall, but I was, as always, very glad to be back in the water. I hate having other people have control over my life, even though the yard workers couldn't have been nicer. The water was very still in the corner of the harbor occupied by the yacht club, sheltered by multiple breakwaters, but I was glad to feel the boat move slightly, nudge the dock, swing away.

I glanced up from a rugby match I was watching on television between the Lions and the Cheetahs—and South Africa is one of the few countries where that is appropriate—and saw through the companionway three masts in a perfect composition, the one on the right slightly higher than the one on the left, the one in the middle a third shorter, all vertical columns of molten light against a background of pewter cloud. Then THE HAWKE OF TUONELA swung and the pattern changed. A life of water.

Cape Town's harbor was much busier than when I was there in 1988 during apartheid and trade embargos. Despite a couple of minor oil spills from ships, which taught me to tie dock lines tight enough so that they did not droop into the water, it was relatively clean for a big commercial port.

The yacht club is in a small triangle off Duncan Dock, a rectangular basin a full nautical mile long and several hundred yards wide. There were more yachts in another small basin at this end of Duncan Dock, though blocked from my view by a ship in an intervening dry dock.

Outside that basin was another big commercial area called Ben Schoeman Dock. Container ships unloaded both there and in Duncan Dock.

West of Duncan Dock was the redeveloped Victoria and Alfred Basin, entered through a separate entrance in the inner breakwater. Fishing boats, the Robben Island tour catamarans, some tugs—though others were moored near the yacht club, and in the summer smaller cruise ships, docked in Victoria and Alfred, as well as a dozen harbor tour yachts.

There was a small new marina down there too, accessible only by waiting for two small swing bridges to open. And a dry dock for commercial vessels up to about 200 feet long, which was usually filled with Asian fishing boats, though I read in the newspaper that their fishing permits were not going to be renewed in order to preserve the local waters for local boats.

The harbor was not especially noisy, but there was a constant hum of activity and machinery. I could usually hear, in addition to the black men who worked on nearby yachts speaking in their languages with many click like sounds, a hissing of steam or air pressure through a hose, and some machinery, perhaps a crane at the container facility, and a diesel engine. And a few birds, terns or gulls.

By far the biggest object in the harbor, dwarfing everything else, including the biggest ships, was a giant oil exploration platform in Duncan Dock. The base was rectangular, rising many stories high, with several levels of machinery and topped by a drilling derrick. The entire structure was tremendous. As a species we are impressive engineers. "The Pride of South Africa" was painted on its side.

I awoke the next morning to the sound of a muffled foghorn in the distance. The main light on the breakwater was more than a mile away. When I looked through the companionway the shore only twenty yards away was barely visible; masts only blurred silhouettes. Diffuse halos of lights in the parking lot and on the clubhouse. A painting by Turner, who was himself that rarest of creatures: a true original who made money.

When by midmorning the fog had burned off I walked the mile and a half to Victoria and Alfred. I had bought a second hand bicycle, but didn't use it when the pavement was wet.

Bicycling in Cape Town was dangerous. I don't know that drivers were any worse than elsewhere, but there were few bicyclists, and drivers weren't expecting them. In the dock area, the perimeter road had a partial shoulder, but I had to cross at bad angles several treacherous railroad spurs leading to the wharves, and was often almost blown off the road by huge trucks. Still I liked to ride, could feel myself using different muscles from walking, and when able to glide through red lights, got into town or to the Victoria and Alfred as quickly as by taxi.

Walking there I looked over as I always did at the city and the mountain.

When my gaze was at eye level I sometimes forgot the mountain, but then I would come around a corner or out of a building and there it was, not looming over the city, but majestic and grand, particularly at dawn and dusk when shadows are long and define shapes. White clouds were spilling over the top as I walked. Rio de Janeiro is more exotic, almost other worldly so, but Cape Town is every bit as beautiful and, perhaps, more livable, and had already joined Sydney as my favorite cities in the world.

The city is mostly white, some yellow and cream, a few touches of light blue and pale turquoise. Mostly low buildings, with three incongruous residential towers at the inland edge and other office towers clustered downtown. Red tile roofs.

The buildings are confined to the lower quarter of the mountain, which starts to rise two miles from the waterfront, although the present waterfront is filled land. At the time of the first Dutch settlement the water's edge was a quarter to a half mile south, near the fort known as The Castle.

The first slope on which there are buildings is gradual; the next quarter of the mountain steeper; and the last half vertical.

With the recent rain, the lower half was green; the top half exposed rock, something like looking at a section of the Grand Canyon, but up instead of down.

Victoria and Alfred is the shopping/restaurant/tourist development at the west end of the harbor, to which I usually cycled or walked every other day to shop for food and to internet, which I suppose is now an acceptable verb.

The development is world class. New buildings blend with converted warehouses and the working parts of the harbor: fishing boat docks, tugs, and dry docks, which provide some character and color. Three hotels. Two movies. Three Internet connections. Forty or fifty restaurants and more than a hundred other shops. Two grocery markets. All of which made life for visiting yachts considerably more convenient that when I was in Cape Town in 1988.

Several weeks passed after our arrival before a taxi driver corrected me on the name. I had been calling the place Victoria and Albert. But he said, and as I discovered was right, it is Victoria and Alfred. Who the hell, I wondered, was Alfred? He was Queen Victoria's son, who officially opened the construction of the breakwater in 1860, which finally made Cape Town into an all weather harbor.

Bent to certain angles, my right wrist was painful from a fall and from working on the boat. One night it bothered me as I was trying to get to sleep and I realized that I did not need to keep to what was formerly my side of the berth and could move to the middle. One of the good things about Carol being gone was that I didn't tangle my feet with hers at the end of the V-berth. That was also one of the bad things about her being gone.

20 *The Good Capsule*

We travel in capsules. Airplanes. Cars. Buses. Ships. Trains.

We enter our capsules like hopeful larvae with vague dreams of butterflies and we exit them moth-eaten. And with undisguised relief. But not always. Some capsules are better than others. Before her flight back to Boston Carol and I left Cape Town at the start of an overland trip around the country on one of the very best capsules, the Blue Train.

The Blue Train had its origins in a fast rail link between Johannesburg and the mail ships leaving Cape Town in the 1920s and became a luxury passenger service at the end of World War II. Quite incredibly the Blue Train, named after the exterior colors of a railway coach in which British royalty toured the country in the 1930s and later adapted for the entire train, is run by the government, and has maintained its standards and reputation pre- and post- as well as during apartheid. Occasionally humanity surprises you.

I had considered riding the Blue Train in 1988 but timing and expense put me off. The favorable exchange rate tipped the scale this time, although even with the rand at 11 to the dollar, the thousand mile 26-hour journey from Cape Town to Pretoria, South Africa's capital thirty miles northeast of Johannesburg, still cost $800 to $1,000 dollars a couple, depending on choice of compartment, of which there were only two: De Luxe and Luxury. Luxury is four feet longer and with a few additional amenities, including a larger bathtub and situated closer to the dining and lounge cars. There were three Luxury compartments per car to four De Luxe. But nothing was second-class. The bathroom fittings in all were 24-carat gold.

By comparison we could have flown from Cape Town to JoBurg—as South Africans call it—for $60, and, of course, have had a completely forgettable experience.

Still I have done most of my traveling on my own boats and am not accustomed to luxury or to people waiting on me. I am even suspicious of it. But I like trains, and so with the windfall of an unexpected income tax refund and I am tempted to say an attitude at age 60 if not now, when?, except that I felt and acted on the same premise at age 30, Carol and I decided to see how, if not the other half, then the other 1% live, and booked a compartment. Luxury, of course.

May 1, the day of our departure, is Labor Day in much of the world. South Africa calls it Workers Day. A notice posted at the Royal Cape Yacht Club advised that electricity would be off for most of the day in the harbor while new transformers were installed. Someone may have thrown the wrong switch, because power was on in the port that morning, but off in the city center a half-mile away, including the railway station.

Luxury began as our taxi pulled to a stop in front of the Blue Train's private entrance at the side of the main terminal. Three men dressed in handsome black and white zebra patterned tunics—zebra like the animals, not football referees—hastened to open doors, inquire our names, check a printed list, ask what of our luggage we wished to have placed in our compartment and what in the baggage van, and usher us into a candle-lit room filled with over-stuffed armchairs and sofas, and tables with carefully arranged arrays of pastries, fruits, and chocolates. At 10:00 in the morning the candles were not standard, but an adaptation to the power cut, for which the young woman seated at a desk who gave us our tickets and compartment assignment profusely and unnecessarily apologized.

Having arrived earlier than most passengers, we retired to nearby armchairs and were hardly seated before another tunic clad man appeared and asked if he could bring us champagne.

Curious to see who the other passengers would be, we watched the reception room fill as the 11:00 a.m. departure neared. After all, the Blue Train has conveyed presidents, royalty, and even supermodels. But as we had already learned May is no longer tourist season in Cape Town, though the climate is like California's and winter is splendid, and our fellow sybarites, with the exception of a party of six Japanese, were mostly South Africans. We looked around and realized that, alas, the beautiful people were us.

At 11:00 a gentleman in a business suit made a short welcoming speech, the essence of which was biblical, "Ask and ye shall receive," and requested that as our names were read we follow an attendant who would escort us to our suites. As we walked, I said to Carol, "For only 80 passengers, this is a long train." Then thought and added, "But with only 6 or 8 per car, it would have to be." And I was not considering the dining car, lounge car, club car, kitchen car, personnel car, power car, and baggage van.

We were greeted at our car by our butler, not porter, who led us along a wood-paneled plush-carpeted corridor to our suite, where he explained the remote control for the window blinds, air conditioning, television and radio. If we wanted to use the CD player we would actually have to take two steps. Never having anticipated the possibility of a CD player, we had not brought any CDs, and would fortunately be spared such exertion.

After showing us the bathroom—Italian marble floor, full-sized bathtub, thick towels, kimonos, and, of course, 24-carat gold plated fittings—he excused himself to attend to other guests. He was a very pleasant man whose age fell somewhere between Carol's generation and mine with a long African name of many consonants, few vowels, and one click sound, who persistently called us "Daddy" and "Momma."

As he closed the door, Carol said, "This is a *very* nice room." It was an understatement. The interior of our suite, as of the entire train, was a warm, soothing blend of wood—as I was later to read: book matched anigré veneer paneling framed by solid birch—of plush fabrics and supple leather, of browns and creams and yellows and, of course, gold.

With our double bed folded behind wood panels, the compartment contained three armchairs, an end table, and a fold-down wood writing table beneath the picture window. The television, which showed closed circuit movies as well as a continuous live view looking down the tracks ahead of the train, was recessed in a panel above closet space and a small, lockable safe. After hanging up a few items, there was nothing to do but retire to our armchairs and prepare to watch the world go by.

Which, on air-sprung suspension, it soon smoothly began to do. For about thirty-five minutes. And then it stopped. Cape Town's suburbs sliding silently past our window were replaced by a stationary white painted cinder block wall at a commuter stop. It was a nice wall. A clean wall. Something like many modern paintings. But like them it soon ceased to be interesting. After a while an announcement came over the intercom that we were making a brief stop to attend to a minor maintenance problem. Noon came and we, having chosen the early sitting for lunch and dinner, made our way to the dining car, passing a small discrete jewelry shop and through the lounge along the way.

Once aboard the Blue Train, there were no additional charges. Everything—except it is noted some foreign wines and spirits, for which read: French champagne, and, though I did not test them, probably single malt scotch—is included. Three meals a day, tea in the afternoon, snacks in the lounge or your suite, and all the South African booze you can possibly keep down. There is also no individual tipping. "Those guests who wish to show their appreciation may leave a gratuity in the box located in the lounge car." Such gratuities being shared by the entire train staff.

The dining car was as elegant as we had already come to expect. Tables for four to one side, tables for two on the other, were set with bone china, fine linen, and silver cutlery. The food and service were excellent. That I don't remember what we ate is not important. I think I had fish for lunch and lamb for dinner; but it may have been the other way around. Whatever we had the meal was pleasant and enjoyable, particularly when the obstinate wall slowly disappeared astern and was replaced by the vineyards near Stellenbosch, which were the source of the wine we were drinking.

As one would expect, South Africa has excellent seafood; but it also has excellent lamb, every bit as good as Australia's and New Zealand's, which is a bit odd because, while in the latter countries sheep are conspicuous, we never saw a single sheep in South Africa, although we criss-crossed the entire country. Surely a matter for conspiracy theorists.

Having dined, we retired to our suite and renewed contemplation of the countryside.

South Africa's wine country is reminiscent of California's Napa Valley but surrounded by more spectacular mountains. May is fall in South Africa and vines change color, so the hillsides rising toward craggy peaks were green and rust and russet.

After a sojourn to the lounge car for midafternoon tea, which we did not need but had because it was there, Carol went on a brief bus tour of Matjiesfontein, the only scheduled stop on the route north.

I am not sure why the train stops at Matjiesfontein, except to give Blue Train passengers a break from the tedium of elegance and comfort. Matjiesfontein is a small desert town, almost a ghost town—the train had climbed through the mountains onto the high arid plateau known as the Great Karoo, whose only claims to fame seem to be that the first international cricket match in South Africa was played there—obviously when it was more thriving—and that the writer, Olive Schreiner, once lived there. Carol said the bus tour was brief and the guide moderately amusing.

Not yet bored with elegance, I remained on board and wallowed in it by taking a bath.

I seldom take baths. Yacht clubs and marinas have showers, and at anchor and at sea we use solar shower bags or buckets of ocean water. I do not even like baths, but, like afternoon tea, the tub was there, so I turned the gold fittings and let it fill with water and stepped in.

After a while a small ripple indicated that the train had resumed its journey. I assumed that Carol was back on board somewhere and added more hot water. The train moves so smoothly that I had not previously noticed the motion, but as we went around a long curve, the water level in the tub titled toward my chin. We were heeled. Barely. But heeled. I felt at home and smiled.

Prior to the journey I had gone to the Blue Train's website, which had alerted me to their request that gentlemen wear a jacket and tie to dinner and so had brought along my only tie and Harris Tweed jacket. More formal wear, it was implied, would not be out of place. It would on me.

As darkness fell over the Great Karoo we made our way back to the dining car, where we found fresh flowers on the tables and subdued lighting. We ate lamb or fish or fish or lamb or beef or chicken, and drank a bottle of South African cabernet sauvignon. No one in the dining car was dressed formally. Carol in a gossamer steel-blue silk blouse and tan skirt and shoes with higher heels than Docksiders, effortlessly fulfilled her responsibilities as the beautiful people. The vastness of the Karoo outside was pin pricked only by an occasional light.

Following an extraordinarily relaxed and pleasant meal, we retired to the lounge for brandy and coffee. The club car in the opposite direction from the lounge is actually more intimate, but is the train's only public smoking area.

When we returned to our suite, a full sized double bed had appeared. Using the remote control, I turned down the air conditioning, and we went to sleep, while the Blue Train glided smoothly through the night.

Awakening early as is my custom, I shaved and dressed without disturbing Carol, and went to the lounge in search of coffee. Breakfast is served between 7:00 and 10:00. At 6:30 I was the only passenger in the lounge, where two of the staff behind the bar were polishing and rearranging glasses. One of them brought a cup of coffee to my armchair, which I sipped as light returned to a changed world.

South Africa is one of the most beautiful countries in the

world, but like the United States it has a necessary, but boring heartland of farmland. If most of the country reminds one of California, the heartland is Missouri, from which I have happily traveled far.

Precisely at 7:00 the Japanese party of six passed through the lounge. We smiled and nodded greetings and I followed them to the dining car where, as always, I was offered much more food than I wanted. The waiter seemed disappointed at my request only for a glass of orange juice and a croissant, although perhaps he brightened when I later returned with Carol and had yogurt and fresh fruit.

In the course of the morning, farm land and wildflowers gave way first to a moonscape of miles of gray mountains of rubble that are the tailings from gold mines, and then to poverty, as we passed shanty towns on the outskirts of Johannesburg. Carol, who had read Nelson Mandela's autobiography more recently than I, recognized names of places of early 1990s violence.

The Blue Train is not a bullet train. Its maximum speed is 70 miles per hour, but during the night it had made up the time lost beside the white wall, and we moved through the suburbs of Johannesburg only a few minutes behind schedule. The view through our window led us to conclude that the richest man in South Africa is the manufacturer of razor wire.

As we approached Pretoria, a discreet knock on the door announced the arrival of our butler, who whisked away our baggage, which magically reappeared beside our rental car in the station parking lot. Of all the Blue Train services, after a lifetime of lugging cumbersome bags and backpacks, this was perhaps the one I appreciated most.

The train stopped, we made our way, hands unencumbered, into the corridor, where we had to pause for a few moments. Earlier I had considered the passing of the Blue Train, an insulated capsule of relative wealth, through the poverty just outside our window. As we stood waiting to disembark I happened to notice through the Venetian blinds that one of the safety windows was shattered as though hit by a rock; so perhaps I was not the only one to have given thought to disparity that morning.

As we stepped down into a sunny Pretoria midday, I realized that The Blue Train is also a time capsule. We had left on Wednesday and now it was Thursday, yet no time seemed to have passed. Perhaps when we returned to Cape Town I would install a bathtub and a butler on THE HAWKE OF TUONELA.

21 *Elephants and the Road*

At the great Limpopo River we turned back.

Earlier that morning we had annoyed several elephants. We hadn't intended to annoy elephants. It was just one of those bad elephant days, sort of a bad hair day that weighs several tons.

We were at the end of a gravel road, ten miles off the two-lane paved road that is the spine of Kruger National Park, at the point where the crocodile infested Luvuvhu joins the mighty Limpopo. Except that in early May, near the start of the dry season, the Limpopo was not mighty. From our rented Mazda, we looked across a wide but shallow river bed of dry sand broken only by a thin trickle of water into Zimbabwe to the north and Mozambique to the south. The division is arbitrary. There is nothing to choose between them. No dwellings. No signs of man. Only a few scattered scruffy trees and some dusty bushes.

On the map the place is suggestively named, "Crook's Corner," and an isolated outpost of the South African police is nearby, though no clues to the nature of the crook's business were evident. Perhaps the place was named after a Mr. Crook. In any event it was a corner and as far as we could go to the northeast and still be in South Africa. THE HAWKE OF TUONELA was more than a thousand miles to the southwest. Like other explorers before us, it was time to start heading home.

We slowly retraced our route along the Luvuvhu, which though smaller and narrower than the Limpopo has cut a deeper bed and sustains more vegetation. As well as more crocodiles.

We had lunched at a designated picnic ground on its banks, one of the places outside the main camps where visitors to

Startled elephants startle sailors. Kruger National Park

Kruger are permitted to leave their cars, though posted with the obligatory signs stating that you do so at your own risk. The grounds were pleasant and the facilities basic, with a few picnic tables, barbecue grills, clean restrooms, and a cheerful young man who sold cold drinks from a cooler.

Most visitors to the park stay in the south as I did on my first visit; the north is much less crowded. We had seen few cars during the morning, and only a few of the other tables were occupied. As we were eating we realized that there was no fence between the grounds and anything that cared to climb the riverbank to nibble our lunch or us. The authorities know what they are doing, we thought. Which is not what six decades of experience with authorities have taught me to expect, but for some reason seemed right at the time. It was only after we had finished lunch and driven for five seconds that we saw bank to bank crocodiles. Perhaps crocodiles don't like to climb. Certainly these were not hungry. They were a sleeping, scaly logjam in the sun. As we watched, two ducks landed and swam nonchalantly past their noses, only a few feet from grinning jaws. So perhaps the authorities do know what they are doing and the crocs are not a problem. Still we were glad we saw them after lunch rather than before.

Ever watchful for elephants, who are amazingly adept at hiding behind blades of grass, we made our way out to the main road and turned west for the Pafuri Gate.

This was our sixth day in the park and that was enough for one visit.

Kruger is 250 miles long and between 20 to 50 miles wide. At a maximum legal speed of 31 miles per hour, we had driven all of the length and much of the width, stayed in three different camps, watched a fiery sun rise over the African plain from the high camp overlooking the Oliphants River, watched the sunset silhouette spiky acacias trees, and had seen all of the big five:

Cheetah auditioning for position as new ship's cat. Stellenbosch, South Africa

lion, leopard, rhino, water buffalo, and—of course, up close and too personal—elephants. And, almost unbelievably, a cheetah, of which there are only 200 in the entire park.

This was far beyond my first experience of Kruger, and was due to better planning: staying in different camps and scheduling two sunset drives by park rangers. Visitors on their own must be back within the main camps before dark.

Along the way we learned that hippopotamuses turn pink in the sun—picture thirty tons of pinkish hippos sleeping in a row on a river bank; that cheetah hunt during the day because they are too small to compete with leopard and lion who hunt at night. And we were reminded that life is simple: it is eating, sleeping, and having sex maybe one week a year. Almost every animal we saw was either doing or contemplating one of the three. The exceptions were three lion cubs we saw playing around their mother in a dry riverbed, and a group of baby hippos who were frolicking in another river near their mothers. The baby hippos really did frolic, splashing, swimming, diving, chasing one another about like any group of kids at a swimming hole.

And then there were the elephants. Elephants in Kruger are pretty much a sure thing. You go to Kruger and you may not see a big cat—there are about 2,000 lions and 1,000 leopards in addition to the 200 cheetahs—but there are 10,000 elephants, as well as over 100,000 impalas. You go to Kruger and you will see elephant and impala.

Elephants are not good conservationists. They are, in fact, profligate, eating only about 20% of what they root up and rip down, and leave 200 pounds of droppings each day. Multiply that by 10,000 and you drive carefully.

Until that last day we got along with elephants. We saw them, stopped the little Mazda, often quite close, and watched them stand, tear branches off trees, chew leaves meditatively, and plod away. But that last day we and the elephants were out of synch.

It began just after we left Shingwedzi camp, where we had stayed overnight, and headed north. Carol saw an elephant off to the left and I hit the brakes. Going only 30 miles an hour, this was hardly a panic stop. But the brakes did squeal slightly. The elephant, a solitary male, took umbrage at this, and squealed loudly, stuck his ears out wide, and charged. The guidebooks say that such charges are only gestures and the elephant will stop before crunching your vehicle. We decided not to see if the elephant had read the same book and hastily drove on.

An hour later and fifteen miles further north, on a twisty, dusty side road, we saw a female elephant with a baby. Again we stopped, and as we watched soon realized that there were several other elephants in the foliage. Except during breeding season, males wander alone or in bachelor groups of two or three, but females stay together in larger herds to raise the young.

The mother we had seen first finally came down a slope and crossed the road in front of us. Her offspring followed tentatively, sliding down the incline with front legs extended like a cartoon, then hurried to catch up with its mother who had already disappeared into the brush on the other side.

Thinking the show was over, we drove up a hill, made a sharp turn to the left, and discovered that it was not. The bulk of the breeding herd—and bulk is the right word—fifteen or twenty elephants of several generations, were peacefully grazing in a small clearing. The nearest was a trunk length away. We were moving at less than 10 miles an hour, but we startled the elephants, of which two young females protectively spun toward us, flared out their ears, raised their trunks, waved their heads from side to side. "We're sorry," we said. "We didn't know you were here." "Ha!" they trumpeted.

An hour later and fifteen or twenty miles further north, we stopped in an area of high grass and scattered trees beside a small river to watch a solitary male munch a tree a safe twenty yards away. After a while, he ambled on, and so did we. But then he made a sharp left turn onto the road and stopped. So did we. The road was only one elephant wide. The elephant looked at us. We looked at the elephant. The elephant appeared thoughtful. The elephant appeared to fall asleep. But finally the elephant began to appear impatient, even anxious. We backed up. The elephant clumped slowly forward. Behind us were miles of narrow, twisty, unpaved road. We wondered how far south this elephant intended to go, but then noticed a break in the bush to our left heading down to the river. Past it we stopped, and the elephant obligingly turned and went down to quench his thirst.

That, we decided, is enough elephants for one day. From now on we won't stop to watch any creature bigger than a vervet monkey.

And that was the last elephant. From there to the Parfuri Gate we saw nothing more threatening than elephant droppings.

At the isolated Parfuri Gate we found a pole across the road and a small shack. After a minute or two a man walked slowly and weakly from the shack. He was emaciated and, despite the heat of the day, bundled in a ragged gray sweater. He was obviously ill and, this being South Africa we thought, AIDS; but malaria is also endemic in the northeast of the country. The man smiled and handed me a clipboard and a pencil. He said something in, I think, Afrikaans. South Africa has eleven official languages, so I'm not sure. Whatever he said, I took the clipboard and signed my name on the form attached. He stumbled to the front of the car and wrote down the license number, then laboriously raised the pole and waved as we drove through.

On the map the gate is shown as being two miles inside the park boundary. The road was straight and paved. We had not seen any animals for quite some time, but were uncertain as to whether we could resume normal speed. After a few miles we decided we were out of the park, "At last," I said, "I won't have to worry about animals in the road." But as I increased our speed to 62 miles an hour and came over a hill to find a cart pulled by three donkeys, I learned that I was quite wrong.

Until we reached what is known as the Garden Route, along the south coast, two hundred miles from Cape Town, we would find people and animals—mostly cattle, but also goats, donkeys, and the occasional baboon or monkey—in the road at irregular and unexpected intervals.

Pedestrian checking the right-of-way. Kruger National Park

We would also find that at 62 miles an hour, which is 100 kilometers an hour, half the traffic whizzed past us—the maximum speed limit is 120 kilometers an hour—and that we would whiz past, when we could pass, the other half, which travels at 35 miles an hour. The first half consisted of big cross country trucks and buses and Mercedes Benz and BMWs driven by presumably affluent whites; the other half consisted of tractors and old Volkswagen and Toyota vans, which serve as public transport in rural areas, driven by blacks. Combine this with driving on the British side of the road, where even if you have spent years living in various parts of the Commonwealth as I have, an American's early conditioning is always wrong; roads in less than perfect repair—I hadn't seen this many potholes since I last drove through the Bronx—with even national highways usually being only two lanes, and you have all the elements of a less than relaxing motoring experience.

We had hardly gone a hundred miles when I thought, "This is a big mistake." Still I wanted to show Carol the country and visit by land some places I had visited by sea fourteen years earlier. And after stopping that first night in Pietersburg, since, I think, renamed, Polokwane, and a long day's drive south through uninteresting farmland, we had survived the worst, and began to enjoy ourselves in a landscape similar to the more attractive parts of the American West, but, perhaps because of a particular quality to the light and certainly because of the people, distinctly African.

The most interesting thing about driving through rural South Africa is that out in the middle of nowhere you see people walking. Now I understand walking. I take pleasure in not owning a car. I walk or ride a bicycle, although I am on the basis of several months' personal observation the only old white man in Cape Town, and perhaps the country, to do so. But in rural areas you see people ten miles from anywhere in any direction walking. We are talking about walking as you read of in the novels of Thomas Hardy or of Abe Lincoln, walking twenty miles to borrow a book. Late on a Friday afternoon, many men were dressed in their best clothes, sport coats and ties, heading we knew not where. And women often were carrying heavy loads balanced on their heads: fire wood; bundles wrapped in cloth; pots; plastic canisters of water.

South of the farmland, we drove into the Drakensburg Mountains, where there are many famous resorts, and, seven miles up an unpaved rock/dirt road, which reduced us to far less than Kruger speed, were fortunate to find a room at the Sani Pass Hotel where we lingered for a pleasant day.

The hotel is located in its own private valley, through which runs a charming stream, and has many possible activities, from golf to mountain biking to 4-by-4 excursions up the Sani Pass to the Kingdom of Lesotho. We opted for nothing more strenuous than a short walk beside the stream and sitting on the terrace, sipping cool drinks, and admiring the surrounding mountains.

Two days later, after passing through what was known as the Transkei and is now simply the Eastern Cape, we again took respite from the road at Knysna on the south coast.

Knysna is situated on a small lagoon, surrounded by timber

country in which the only one or two free range elephants left in South Africa are reputed to live. For many years there was thought to be just one, but recently another had been sighted. I am pleased to say not by us.

I had sailed into Knysna fourteen years earlier. The entrance through two narrow rocky headlands is spectacular, but RESURGAM's exit was something more.

After waiting for two days for a storm to pass and with a favorable weather forecast, we had left a mooring at the small yacht club and powered a mile to the headlands, where we were dismayed to find three lines of breaking waves. I circled twice, studying the waves. A hundred yards beyond them the ocean was smooth all the way to Cape Town. I thought I saw an interval and headed out. I was wrong, and the boat was swept end to end before we emerged wet and happy on the other side. I don't like to rely on engines, yet there were a few seconds when if the diesel had died, so probably would we. That we did not resulted in an adrenaline rush I could still feel as Carol and I drove to the headlands and looked out and found waves breaking there still.

22 **Becoming an Old Poem in Winter**

The Cape of Storms became the cape of storms.

The storms were not continuous and generally passed quickly, with a day or two of gale force wind and rain and temperatures around 50°F followed by a day or two of warmer sunshine before another front came through. Although the water at the yacht club remained smooth, two of the gales built waves that crashed over the breakwaters and closed the harbor. In one of them a ship dragged anchor in Table Bay and drifted to within a hundred yards of shore before the crew could get her underway.

One front that was moderate when it passed through Cape Town stalled and intensified in the eastern half of the country, causing snowfalls in inland KwaZulu Natal. South African buildings aren't designed for this and roofs collapsed. Places Carol and I had driven through on our way back from Kruger looked for a few days like New England in January.

Two ships got into trouble off the coast. One had lost power, was taking on water, and couldn't use its pumps. Television talking-heads kept saying the other was on a sandbar, while showing footage of a vessel aground in surf a ship's length from a beach, which I suppose can be called a sandbar.

No explanation was given as to how the ship got there. Perhaps she too lost power. It was reported that the captain had had a heart attack and was removed by helicopter. It was not reported whether he had the heart attack before or after the grounding.

People around the yacht club complained about the cold, although temperatures seldom dropped below 50°F and the lowest I noted in THE HAWKE OF TUONELA's cabin all winter was 44°F. To a New Englander, even a transplanted and reluctant one, Cape Town was sometimes a bit raw, but never cold.

Between storms I worked on the boat, repainting the nonskid deck and searched for two irritatingly ineradicable leaks, one around the mast, the other around the companionway. No matter how closely and minutely I examined the areas, I could not find the sources. I finally had some success by spreading sealant over many unlikely spots, but had no confidence that the leaks would not reappear at sea. In this, I was unfortunately prescient.

In all but the worst weather, even in intermittent rain, the black men caring for nearby boats polished stainless steel and scrubbed decks. The cost of labor was very low.

They spoke to one another mostly in Xhosa/Zulu.

I found South Africa a surprisingly multilingual society. Many people moved seamlessly between English and Afrikaans, and some to Xhosa/Zulu as well. Of the eleven official languages, those three were the most common. The SABC broadcast news and other programs in each language on its various channels.

More blacks seemed to speak Afrikaans in addition to their tribal dialect than English, perhaps because under apartheid, they had to. On Robben Island, where political prisoners were held, they could only send and receive letters written in Afrikaans. And were permitted only one or two letters a year.

Before she returned to Boston, Carol and I took the catamaran ferry to Robben Island.

In 2001 visitors were guided by former prisoners, many of whom had been released less than ten years earlier. I was struck by how much worse the rank and file prisoners were treated than were the leaders, with three hundred men living in a room that should have held perhaps twenty. And the countless small indignities. Prisoners were divided into three groups: white, colored, and black. Whites and colored were issued long pants; blacks shorts. Boys wear shorts. Men wear pants. The message was clear.

Being in South Africa in 2001 was like being in the United States about 1800. The founding fathers were dying off. Three historic ANC leaders died in the months after our arrival, but George Washington in the form of Nelson Mandela was still around, although he was using a cane. He featured much more in the news than did the actual president, Thabo Mbeki.

AIDS in South Africa was strange. News reports said that more than 20% of the population was HIV positive, and that in the preceding two years the life expectancy for South Africans had dropped from 54 years to 37 for women and 38 for men. In neighboring Botswana 60% of the women admitted to hospitals to give birth were HIV positive.

I didn't doubt the statistics, but I thought of Defoe's *Journal of the Plague Year* and Camus' *The Plague* and wondered, "Where are the bodies?" A steady stream of carts heaped high with corpses should be trundling down darkened streets every night. AIDS was killing as many people as the Black Death, yet remained invisible. Though perhaps not in the townships and rural areas.

I found South Africa to be perhaps the most interesting and important social experiment going on in the world. With great natural resources, the soundest infrastructure on the continent, politicians not yet more corrupt than politicians everywhere, tribalism, some obscene superstitions (among them the belief that having sex with an infant can cure AIDS), a great many people of good will of all races were trying to create a truly multiracial society, while neighboring Zimbabwe had become the most Orwellian country on the planet. Everything in South Africa would depend on succession and avoidance of a demagogue.

Reconciliation was institutionalized as a national holiday, and most people seemed to have risen above revenge and simply wanted to get on with life.

Crime in South Africa received publicity, but in Cape Town I felt no more at risk than I would have in Boston or any other major city. Everyone in Cape Town, of all races, said that crime was much worse in JoBurg.

I settled back into solitude almost as complete as if I were at sea, working on the boat, reading, listening to music, writing. Many days I did not speak a single word, going ashore only to shower.

I still found myself pumping the foot pump in the galley seven times into the teakettle for coffee, which is the number for both Carol and me, and then having to pour some out. For myself I needed only four pumps.

I continued to ride my bicycle or walk to Victoria and Alfred every other day.

One day something reminded me of a poem I had written in Tahiti thirty years earlier, during one of the times I was waiting for Suzanne. It was about a solitary old man I often saw riding a blue bicycle along the Papeete waterfront. I realized that I had become my poem. Just as I became a different poem, "Gray Days," when I sank RESURGAM. I was about the same age the old man was then, and I was riding a blue bicycle. Different waterfront.

There were buskers at Victoria and Alfred, mostly musicians and groups of a cappella singers in the tradition of Ladysmith Black Mambazo, the group that gained wealth and fame as backup singers on Paul Simon's "Graceland"—in which was the great line: "Every generation sends a hero up the pop charts."

Performers had to audition in order to work the waterfront and the quality was high.

Not all the music was African. A quintet of middle-aged black men playing Dixieland jazz would have been at home on the streets of New Orleans. But all, with a single exception, were loud.

One young man, who was almost always there when I went over, sat by himself, softly strumming a guitar and singing sweetly. He was good, but no one who wasn't standing right next to him could hear him. His voice was lost in the ambient noise, people talking, cars, a few delivery trucks, boats, cell phones. He was wrong for the venue. I hoped he sang for the love of singing.

On days when I had too much to carry or the weather was inclement, I rode in taxis and tried to learn what I could from the drivers, almost all of whom were black. A few were Malay or Indian. Only two were white, both men about my own age who had never done anything else. And only one was a woman.

A good proportion spoke only minimal English, but I asked those I could converse with where they came from and how life was for them. The majority had moved to Cape Town from the Eastern Cape, where they said there was no work. All said that life was hard, that it was hard to get money. Many said that they had been apprehensive when apartheid ended. They had been afraid the ANC would be too radical. Transitions are always hard.

The drivers did not own their cabs, but rented them from companies or individual owners. During the summer tourist season business was better, but in winter when I rode back from Victoria and Alfred in early afternoon, most drivers told me that I was their first or second fare of the day, after a five or six hour wait.

The taxis had meters, but the meters varied considerably over the same distance, sometimes in favor of the passenger. The ride from Victoria and Alfred to the RCYC was sometimes 30 rand and sometimes 50. One day the meter read only 12 rand. The driver didn't even notice. I gave him 40 rand and told him he should have the company fix his meter, which was costing him money. One $4 fare every six hours, and not all that is profit.

If you own your own boat and have a little money you possess a freedom of wealth unimaginable to most of the people in the world and a freedom of time unknown to billionaires.

23 *Not the Vision*

On August 1 Carol moved into her condominium, and two weeks later, my work on THE HAWKE OF TUONELA completed, I flew back to see what she had wrought.

On August 16 we celebrated our eighth wedding anniversary and the tenth anniversary of my coming dripping from the water after I sank RESURGAM.

I sat looking out the window that morning. I had never expected to see Charlestown again, much less live there.

The condo is only a few blocks from the marina where we had lived and from which we had sailed a little more than a year earlier. Carol was fashioning a pleasant nest. A few days earlier she had bought an antique Persian carpet. For our anniversary I bought a Tiffany bud vase to replace the one I once gave to her that had remained on the boat. The new vase sat in the opening between the kitchen and the dining area, filled with yellow sunflowers and a big purple daisy.

Several new buildings had gone up near the marina. A hotel was under construction on Frederic Tudor's old wharf.

I saw familiar faces when I walked down the street. Not people I knew personally, but recognized as being Charlestown regulars. As perhaps they recognized me and briefly wondered where I had been. And I thought: all the time I've been gone, the hundred days at sea, Portugal, Dakar, Brazil, Cape Town, they've been here, doing the same things day after day. It was a familiar thought, even more striking in the past when I returned to San Diego after almost dying at sea a time or two.

Charlestown's streets are narrow and irregular. The buildings red brick and mostly three and four stories high and residential, except for the new hotel and offices by the waterfront that rise to six or seven stories and the old Five Cent Savings Bank building. At Five Cents "old" is redundant. At street level are several restaurants, a florist, dry cleaners, a hair salon. Directly across from my window is Sullivan's Pub.

This is the gentrified side of Charlestown, which had been populated for a hundred years by Irish laborers. While the streets are narrow, the sidewalks, also red brick, are wide. About every ten yards alternate gas light lamps and trees that in August are in full greenery. The condo is effectively on the third floor, and the upper branches of a tree were just outside some of the windows. It is an attractive, convenient urban setting, and Carol seemed happy there.

The condo is small—660 square feet Carol tells me; I have no idea of how to judge such things—one bedroom, a living/dining room, kitchen, bath; and expensive. Two days earlier in the newspaper I saw that the average residence in Boston costs over half a million dollars. I also saw a typically self-congratulatory opinion piece on the editorial page titled with absurd naïveté/arrogance, "It doesn't get much better than Boston!" I felt fragmented. What passes, as "the real world" seemed unreal to me.

We bought many things, from a television and DVD player and stereo equipment to furniture.

Boston had a heat wave of nine consecutive days above 90°F. As unaccustomed to the heat as polar bears, Bostonians were melting. A doctor was amazed that I had walked to his office downtown for a routine exam in the heat. It was closer than walking to Victoria and Alfred.

Over the Internet I ordered some boat equipment that was easier to obtain in the U.S. than South Africa.

Other than being with Carol, having full Internet access was probably the thing I liked most about being back in the U.S. Followed by a flushing toilet, hot water, and Fox Sports World on cable television, which carried more soccer than even I wanted to watch, with games from England, Germany, Brazil and

Argentina, and even the tri-nations rugby, where South Africa upset Australia in a match played in Cape Town.

September 11 was the first anniversary of the terrorist attacks on the World Trade Center and the Pentagon. It was also the day Carol's cleaning woman came, so I walked downtown and wandered through bookstores and then spent time in the library. Armed and nervous policemen were on every corner.

A year earlier we were in Vilamoura, Portugal.

A few days later I was at Logan Airport, looking out at a gray sky and a gray sliver of water toward Winthrop, where Sylvia Plath once lived. A low peninsula. White buildings, green trees, one yellow tower of unknown purpose, small boats on moorings in olive/brown water; planes landing in the foreground: rain running down terminal windows.

When I first sailed to Boston in 1989, while Jill and I were separated, I keep RESURGAM on a mooring off Winthrop; and THE HAWKE OF TUONELA spent part of her first summer in New England in 1995, the year after Carol and I were married, anchored there.

The September sky was gray. Wintry looking, though in fact the moisture had come up from the south and the day was not cold. Still it was a sky from which one could expect snow to fall. And in a few months it would.

My flight to Amsterdam, where I would make the connection to Cape Town, was not due to depart for three hours. Carol had driven me over early and we had lunch before she had to go to a meeting.

I had had no problems with airport security, though I thought I might. My carry-on bag was filled with boat electronics that could easily arouse suspicion. Two cockpit stereo speakers, a tillerpilot, a panel to show battery voltage, a repaired display for the instrument system, a GPS. Lots of wires and odd shapes. Nevertheless it passed through the X-ray machine without causing comment. Old men don't arouse much suspicion. The only old men who are dangerous are politicians and generals.

Logan continued to be a disorganized, poorly designed,

unuser friendly, forever-under-construction mess. About as bad as a big airport can be. Schipol Airport in Amsterdam makes it look like a slum. But then so does a slum.

I glanced around the crowded terminal and wondered who are all these people and why are we all in motion?

An oriental food stall in the food court named, "Wok and Roll."

A pretty teen aged girl with some sort of palsy being pushed in a wheel chair by her mother, moving determinedly from the wheel chair to a chair at a table, ignoring yet aware of the attention she drew. She didn't want sympathy; she wanted a different fate.

And the next day at Schipol in Holland: a T-shirt worn presumably by one of my fellow countrymen with big letters: FDNY, for Fire Department New York. Above them, "United We Stand," and below them, "These Colors Don't Run."

Finally after two endless flights I was back aboard THE HAWKE OF TUONELA in Cape Town under a full moon. In Boston I never saw the moon. I was so glad to be back in Cape Town, so glad to see Table Mountain through the companionway, so glad to be back on the boat.

I was not alive in Boston. Carol's place is pleasant. We joked about my sitting in a wheelchair by the window when I am older and senile, looking down on Main Street, watching people pass, changing stations on the television with the remote control. I suppose it could happen.

But for me it was not life. Certainly not the vision I had.

I provisioned the boat, gave my electric heater to one of the black boat workers, gave my bicycle to one of the yacht club's security guards, got a 5,000-mile haircut, and went to sea.

24 Hard Water

I heard the wave coming, hissing like a snake, but then I had heard many waves coming. Seven or eight every minute. Even when I did not hear them approach, they sometimes suddenly exploded against the hull like artillery shells. Several had picked us up and thrown us far over. Countless had filled the cockpit and poured through the edges of the companionway. The sodden chart of the Southern Ocean between Africa and Australia had long been removed from the chart table. Twice I had been completely soaked in the cabin and now wore foulweather gear inside even with the companionway closed.

THE HAWKE OF TUONELA and I were 2,200 miles and five storms out of Cape Town at 41°S, 59°E. That Carol had returned to her architectural career before this passage was additional, though redundant, proof of her superior intelligence.

The instrument system had recorded maximum gusts in these storms of 57, 60, 44, 51, and 61 knots of apparent wind coming from astern, so the true wind was several knots greater. This wave spared me the annoyance of reading such numbers again.

While a gale near land is always dangerous, I have my own version of the Beaufort Scale for storms in the open ocean: 30-40 knots from astern is good sailing; 40-50 worrying; 50-60 damaging; 60+ I wish I were somewhere else.

I was sitting on the starboard settee berth, facing aft, trying to concentrate on David McCullough's fine biography of John Adams. THE HAWKE OF TUONELA was making six to seven knots under bare poles—and it can probably be stated categorically that if you can do seven knots under bare poles, you should be under bare poles—the Monitor steering. This is pushing the limit of what can be expected of a vane steering gear. But if I had taken the helm myself every time the waves reached 20 feet, I would have been sitting out there most of the past two weeks, now a small, shriveled, exhausted prune.

Seven waves a minute is 10,000 every twenty-four hours. Of 10,000, one or two or three are going to break at precisely the wrong instant. It is surprising that it does not happen more frequently.

I felt the wave pick us up and flip us onto our beam. I slid sideways up the backrest toward the overhead. I watched and heard water flood over the stern. Two plastic canisters of miscellaneous screws and bolts flew from beside the port quarter-berth across the cabin to smash into the door of the hanging locker to starboard.

I have turned a boat the size of THE HAWKE OF TUONELA over three times at sea, twice on my first circumnavigation not far from our current position. Almost everything is secured in the cabin, but when I had added a third battery in Cape Town, I re-arranged the area beside the quarter berth and left these canisters loose. Had this knockdown occurred at night, they would have passed close to my head. Once I was hit in the head during a capsize by Adlard Coles' book, *Heavy Weather Sailing*. The canisters would have hurt more.

The wave dropped us. Our keel and the law of gravity turned us upright. I put John Adams down and waded aft, through water gushing through the closed companionway, glanced out to see if the Monitor was still steering. A wave in one gale had snapped a control line, while a wave in another had broken the wind vane paddle. I used to think that you could not work on deck in 60 knots of wind, but in fact, as I had proven hanging over the stern rethreading a line through the vane tube to the servo rudder as we rose and fell twenty or thirty feet, if you have to you can. Satisfied that the Monitor was intact, I bent to capture the rolling canisters, which to the manufacturer's credit had not broken, and took them forward to a locker with a latch on it, and returned to restore some order in the main cabin.

Moderating wave in Southern Ocean. When conditions were rougher I couldn't take photographs

Books from the shelf to port had dropped onto the upper berth to starboard, other books and manuals had fallen from the shelf beside the starboard quarterberth. Cushions, liferaft, ditch bag were in a jumble. The long unused Air Sight Reduction Tables swam across the cabin sole in pursuit of a Yanmar owner's manual, a West Marine catalog, and broken slats from the door. I fished them out and dropped them on the chart table.

The digital battery readout showed the house batteries to be in free fall. Voltage was 12.20 and dropping. I flipped the switch and found the third battery steady at 12.70.

Moving handhold to handhold, for despite the extra ballast of a cockpit full of water THE HAWKE OF TUONELA was still being thrown around, I checked the instrument system readout. It was blank. I turned the system off, then on again. Nothing. I turned it off. The batteries were now at 12.12.

THE HAWKE OF TUONELA has a bolt-on keel and a very shallow bilge. Three or four gallons of water are enough to slosh over the sole when the boat is heeled 15° or 20°, and there were now considerably more than four gallons of water, and as we continued to slide down big waves we were variously heeled considerably more than 20°.

The electric bilge pump is ineffective against this darting water, besides I did not want to run anything from the batteries, so I moved the table from where it is secured to the mast—tied on one side because I had broken the hook when I lurched against it several days earlier—lifted the floorboard, and set to work with hand pump and bucket.

Each time I partially opened the companionway to empty the bucket, the water in the cockpit was lower. By the time I dumped my final, fifth bucket, it was empty.

Pools of water had collected on the upper starboard berth. I sponged them up. The television, covered routinely by a plastic trash bag and well secured by straps, sat in a pool like a statue about to be unveiled in a fountain. After five months in Cape Town everything had been in perfect order aboard the boat at our departure; now the list of items damaged was twenty and climbing, and I wondered if anything, perhaps including me, was going to survive.

Another knockdown a few days earlier had caused me to review abandon ship procedure. I thought if I had ten minutes I could get into Carol's liferaft, which she had bequeathed me, well enough prepared to survive a long, miserable time. If I had only five minutes, prolonged survival was problematical. And I was thousands of miles from anywhere.

In an hour, THE HAWKE OF TUONELA's cabin was restored to what had come to pass as normal. A plastic trash bag duct taped over the broken locker door was the only visible sign of the knockdown. The cabin sole was wet, but then the cabin sole was always wet.

I turned on the instrument system again. Numbers appeared, disappeared, appeared, then disappeared.

I took off my wet shoes and socks, added the socks to the trash bag of clothes too soaked to put in the laundry bag, changed into dry socks and sea boots and, already wearing foulweather gear, went on deck. Automatically I glanced at the mast-head Windex. Only a stub was standing. The direction vane was also missing from the electronic masthead unit, but the anemometer cups were spinning. Not until I tried to turn on the masthead light that night would I learn that it too was missing and be certain that we had put the masthead in the water.

In Cape Town I had installed an expensive LED in the mast-head to reduce power consumption. It worked very well and was supposed to last 100,000 hours. I was about 99,850 hours short, but somehow did not expect that this would be covered under warranty.

Partially blocked in the troughs, on the crests of waves the wind, which on the last recording had been 59 knots, staggered me. I pulled myself aft to examine the Monitor, which is the most important piece of equipment on the boat. It seemed undam-aged, the control lines unchaffed. Turning forward I checked the deck and rig. Nothing unusual.

Before ducking below I glanced about the ocean. It was a scene of undeniable grandeur. A half dozen albatross with 8-foot wingspans and more than a dozen smaller shearwaters glided and dipped over the peaks and troughs of thousand yard long waves that gleamed in bright sunshine. There had been little rain in any of these storms, usually just a brief ten minute burst when the front passed, followed by a quick wind shift from northwest to southwest and a rising barometer.

One of the things I have sought at sea is purity, and here it was: unblemished beauty and power, perhaps too much power. A shadow loomed over me. I held tight to the grab rail near the main traveler. A week earlier a wave had bent a similar 1-inch stainless tube on which a solar panel was mounted. This wave broke, slamming into my back. When it passed I turned. Of course another wave was coming, but I had time to get below.

Back in the specious security of the cabin, the barometer was panting, its tongue hanging out, exhausted from sprinting up and down the millibars for two weeks. "I can't take any more," it gasped. "1020 one night; 998 the next morning; 1022 a day later. Can't you do something?"

With sympathy for the poor barometer, THE HAWKE OF TUONELA, and, for that matter myself—because the constant tension of waiting for the wave that would breach the hull or bring down the mast and turn this from a six week passage into a twelve week ordeal was wearing—I carefully removed the damp atlas of pilot charts from inside the chart table. Turning its weakened pages as though they were rare parchment, I found the chart for November.

As I studied it I asked myself: what is the purpose of this exercise? And answered: To make as enjoyable a passage between South Africa and Australia as possible with the least amount of drama. In this we had thus far been spectacularly unsuccessful. I was cold and wet and tired and there had been way too much drama. Time and speed did not matter. I was not racing. My days of setting records are long over. A boat the size of THE HAWKE OF TUONELA could expect to cover the 5,000 miles in about six weeks. A fast passage would be five weeks; a slow one seven. A week or two made no difference to my life. If the pilot chart could be believed, between 35°S and 40°S the westerlies still dominated and the percentage of gales would be halved. We were taking too much of a beating. If we ever got out of survival mode and regained some control over our course, I decided to ease north.

Two weeks earlier on my last night in Cape Town I had gone to sleep uncertain that I would get away the next morning. A strong southeast wind came up, which would make leaving the dock difficult if not impossible, but it died just after midnight. I woke at 4:30, got up, made coffee and started the final preparations for sea, cranking some tension onto the backstay, putting handles in winches, hooking up the tillerpilot.

At 6:00 in the flat calm and glassy water I wanted, I tossed the dock lines onto THE HAWKE OF TUONELA, stepped aboard, and backed out of the slip.

Fifteen minutes later I was at the entrance to the breakwater, having passed a seal that at first I mistook for a plastic bag and two bobbing penguins. As I turned to the west I crossed ahead of a tug towing a barge. Seven or eight ships were at anchor in

Table Bay, waiting their turn to enter the harbor. Long swell from the southwest. Cats-paws on the water.

I looked over at Cape Town and Table Mountain. I had come to feel at home there and would miss the place.

Under power I cleared Green Point and turned south about a mile offshore. Although the forecast was for the temperature to rise to 80°, I was cool when the sun went behind high scattered clouds.

An enormous pod of small dolphins passed, leaping between the shore and THE HAWKE OF TUONELA. Hundreds streaming south. A solid mass that took twenty minutes to move beyond us.

A line of mist rose from breakers on the rocks off Camps Bay. Gannets glided in the sky. Several bigger dolphins swam near the boat, breathing just behind and beside us, almost a gasp for air. Seals stuck their heads up to watch us. From the east I could not see Table Mountain, which was blocked by the peaks known as The Apostles.

With the tillerpilot steering under power, I ducked into the cabin for a handful of trail mix, and saw Carol's photo, appealing and touching, on the bulkhead. It was 2:00 a.m. in Boston. She might wake up and wonder if I had left. She wouldn't know with certainty until noon her time when there was no e-mail.

In midmorning I saw what I thought to be Cape Point ahead, but soon realized that it was another light on a point well north. A big sailboat powered past heading north. I raised the mainsail, which didn't help much. I was still dragging out equipment that I hadn't used in a while, including snatch blocks for the preventer on the boom.

At noon Table Mountain again became visible, now to the northeast. I put on sunscreen, though this didn't figure to be a sunscreen passage. THE HAWKE OF TUONELA startled a seal sleeping on his side, one fin in the air, near a clump of drifting kelp. We were beside him before he woke, big brown eyes wide with alarm, and dove.

Finally at 3:00 p.m. I was able to turn off the engine and start sailing. The wind was not in the predicted southeast, but north, a good angle for us.

At sunset we were fifteen miles south of Cape Point. Running lights of three ships, all well inshore, were in view. Probably my last land and ships for 5,000 miles.

I have made four or five passages longer than this one, the longest being five months, three of them south of 40°S, and 20,000 miles during my first circumnavigation, and I have sailed tens of thousands of miles alone; but not lately.

In the event, it was easy to be alone again in the monastery of the sea.

While anchoring and docking are easier with two people than one, at sea on THE HAWKE OF TUONELA only poling out the jib with the spinnaker pole and lowering the spinnaker sleeve require more than two arms, and with planning these are doable alone. I have often wondered why we didn't evolve as three or four armed creatures, which clearly would seem to have survival advantages, particularly while sailing. Perhaps such a creature couldn't run fast enough.

One evening during the passage I heard on the BBC a researcher say that on average people speak 5,000 to 6,000 words a day. Since Carol returned to her career, I doubt that in port I speak more than a hundred, so it was not much different to be at sea, where I spoke 0 to 10—the 10, if spoken, being expletives as needed.

I was glad in the worst of the weather that I did not have a means of outside communication. Had I been able to talk to Carol each day I would have either had to lie and say that conditions were better than they were or worry her unnecessarily about things she could do nothing about.

There are many ways to divide a long passage. Distance: 5,000 miles. Time: six weeks, plus or minus one. Way points: two: one off Cape Agulhas, which I passed well south of and deleted the second day out; and one off Rottenest Island, ten miles west of Fremantle. Longitude: almost one hundred degrees: Cape Town is 18°E, Fremantle 115°E. Time zones: seven geographically, though only six politically because Cape Town which should be GMT+1 is GMT+2.

In addition I counted weeks' runs; the midway point, which came eighteen days out, and was the midpoint in time as well as distance for Rottenest Island was in sight on the afternoon of day thirty-six; the antipodean point from Boston, 109°E, passed on day thirty-four; and my 61st birthday, November 11, which was pleasant but saw the shortest day's run of only 97 miles under high pressure, with 1,300 miles to go. A year earlier Carol and I had been off the northwest coast of Africa sailing between Gibraltar and Dakar.

During the storms, which began three days and 450 miles southeast of Cape Town, I did not even think of Fremantle, but only of the next fragment of the voyage. At the halfway point we had had six storms and I thought: only six more to go. But the move north worked and in the second half, although the odd wave continued to growl and whap us with a passing paw, we only had two.

Time zones could almost be felt. Dawn and sunset, which along with the wind dominated the rhythm of my life, came an hour earlier, then gradually shifted, until in four or five days they leapt forward again.

I did not have the satisfaction of marking each day's position on the chart and watching the Xs march along. Too many waves made their way below. First removed from the chart table and finally falling apart in my hands, the chart did not make it through the third week. Except for two isolated specks of land, Amsterdam and Saint Paul's Islands, it was empty anyway.

40°S is an artificial border, but for THE HAWKE OF TUONELA it was a valid one. When, after one more storm whose wind I can only estimate to have been at least 60 knots because the tops of more waves were being blown off than in any of our other storms and the sea was whiter and the air filled with more spray, we moved back into the Thirties. The terrible battering ended, and we experienced something like a cold trade wind passage, usually sailing at speed under poled out jib. A final gale two weeks later fell into the good sailing category.

Improved conditions outside saw improved conditions inside. I stopped wearing long underwear; I stopped rigging plastic bags over the head and foot of my berth; I put one of my damp pair of Levis in the cockpit until they became less damp, if not dry. The day came when I was even able to sail with the companionway open; and I didn't have to pump the bilge every six hours or even every day.

The batteries had inexplicably stopped their free fall at 11.80 volts, and began to accept a charge from the one permanently mounted solar panel. When I put the other two panels on deck, I discovered that one of them had no output; but with the other in place, battery voltage increased so that I could check out the electronics, and music returned to my wet little world of books, wind, sea, my own scribbled words and memories.

The chart plotter continued to acquire positions slowly; the radar worked; half the cabin lights were out on the starboard side of the main cabin. Attempts to find the cause were not successful. I needed to remove the overhead to check wiring, and that would have to wait for port.

Rewiring the instrument system to a different on/off switch resulted in some of the displays showing some numbers. We seemed to have heading, seawater temperature, and possibly depth; but no boat speed or wind.

I missed the masthead Windex. For days I found myself glancing at the masthead only to find a disappointing and uninformative stub. I tied tell tails to the shrouds, but still habitually looked at the Windex first.

Birds followed us into the Thirties, soaring around the boat, sometimes landing ahead and watching us sail by. In light wind one day I heard three floating albatross clack their beaks at one another, making a sound similar to the African "click" languages, before one unexpectedly brayed like a sheep. Presumably he had spent time near New Zealand.

The full moon returned as we steadily reduced the distance to Australia by almost a thousand miles a week, the outline of whose coast finally appeared on the right hand side of the chart plotter screen. One night I went on deck to furl the jib after a brief shower and saw ahead of us something I had never seen before which can only be described as a moonbow: a complete ghostly white arch against the stars that would have been a rainbow in sunlight.

Four hundred miles offshore, the wind moved forward of the beam, then continued to the bow and strengthened until we were close hauled on starboard in 20-30 knots. Water over the deck again. And over the floorboards. Plastic bags again rigged over my sleeping bag. Radio Australia broadcast strong wind warnings along the coast day after day as a stationary trough just offshore deepened, until on the day we would make landfall, it predicted the trough would finally move inland with gusts to 45 knots in thunderstorms.

Because I knew we would not reach port before sunset, I slowed THE HAWKE OF TUONELA to four knots under deeply reefed main and a scrap of jib, and watched a spectacular cloud show. Great thunderheads turned into anvils all about us. Lightning. Distant thunder. Then sped east. But none passed directly over us, and in late afternoon a blur on the horizon off our starboard bow firmed into Rottenest Island. I let us approach until sunset, when I turned back out to sea. Fremantle and the end of the hardest passage I had made in more than a quarter century could wait for dawn.

25 West Oz

They call it Oz, and from seaward the office towers of Perth ten miles inland up the Swan River rising from a flat landscape that stretches forever, that stretches to the Never Never, does look like the Wizard's home at the end of Dorothy's yellow brick road. They also call it the "lucky land" and it is that too, a thin smear of sand between a turquoise sea and a big sky, far from most of the troubles of the world.

I had sailed to Australia many times, but I had always been in the east and north of the country. In this I was like most Australians, who live in the southeast and fly off to the U.S. and Europe, but never go west. Perth is the most isolated city with a population of more than one million in the world. Other Australians know it is there because Perth has athletic teams, millionaires who bought up chunks of Sydney in the 1980s, a notorious political scandal, and it was the site of the 1987 America's Cup; but those are not sufficient enticements actually to visit the place.

The city, along with its port, Fremantle, at the mouth of the Swan, is often compared with San Diego. In many ways the comparison is apt. Both are located in the southwest of their respective countries on the edge of great deserts. Both have fine climates. But San Diego has become much larger. Perth at the end of 2002 reminded me of San Diego thirty years earlier. The pace of life in Perth is more comfortable, less crowded. The ocean is bluer and warmer. And outside the city are a thousand miles of deserted beaches instead of Los Angeles.

There are a million and a half people in and around Perth. There are only a few hundred thousand more in all of West Australia, which comprises almost half the entire continent. Perth's and Fremantle's residents know how fortunate they are and, except for those in the tourist industry, are quite satisfied to be ignored by the rest of the country and keep their secret.

In five hard weeks I had sailed not just between two of my favorite countries, but between two of the most hospitable yacht clubs in the world, The Royal Cape and the Fremantle Sailing Club. But before I got to the latter, in what may be a sign of the times, I had to run a gauntlet of bureaucracy and endure the most invasive Customs inspection anywhere ever. Four previous entries into Australia had been routine. The country has strict agricultural regulations, as does New Zealand, which I understand and respect. But my entry into Fremantle was something else.

The timing of my arrival in Fremantle was even more critical than usual. I was in Sydney in 1987 and watched on television what may have been the most exciting America's Cup races of our time thanks to the Fremantle Doctor, the strong wind that blows regularly every afternoon when cool air is pulled in off the ocean by hot air rising from the heated land. I wanted to complete clearance and get THE HAWKE OF TUONELA settled at the Sailing Club before the Doctor called.

Powering past Rottenest Island at first light, I called Fremantle Harbor control on my only radio, a handheld VHF, several times until about four miles from the breakwater entrance, I was within range and they responded. Fremantle Harbor is not large, but it has a complicated breakwater system, with three separate basins for yachts and fishing boats located just south of the commercial port, and I wanted to know exactly where I should go to meet the officials. I was directed to a dock in the southern basin near the Sailing Club. In smooth water and light wind I happily reached it just after 8:00 a.m., thinking I would be cleared in an hour or two at the latest and move HAWKE long before the wind came up. Five hours and thirty knots of wind later I actually did move.

In the intervening time nine officials and a large black dog went over THE HAWKE OF TUONELA with impressive thoroughness. The first of those officials, a man from Customs, could almost cause one to dislike bureaucrats. He was surly, rude and arrogant. Perhaps he had lost a fight with his wife that morning and I was the first person on whom he could take out his frustrations. The only good thing that can be said of him is that he was unAustralian. All the other officials, and the dog, were courteous and simply did their job. The dog even wagged its tail as it climbed onto the chart table and inadvertently ripped up the local chart with its claws. They removed every moveable object, including crawling into the stern and taking an old working jib I keep as a spare onto the dock and unfolding it, something I myself have not done for several years. I was pleased to see that it hadn't become as moldy as I expected.

At one point four Customs agents and two agricultural inspectors were onboard at the same time. This is several more bureaucrats than THE HAWKE OF TUONELA's capacity and they bumped into one another in a scene from a Keystone Cops movie.

It is true that I arrived in Australia only a few months after the terrorist bombing in Bali and, I was told by the lead agent, only a month after a French yacht was found off the coast with a load of drugs. Ah, as Brits say, *the French.* But it must have been evident fairly quickly that I was neither a terrorist nor a drug runner, and I think that I was probably used as a training exercise on a slow day at the office. Ultimately the lead agent became a bit embarrassed, apologized for his people taking so long, and thanked me for my patience.

They did their best to put everything back in place, but on a boat everything has an exact place where it must fall easily to hand when you are awakened by an emergency in the middle of the night; and for several months afterwards I was not finding objects quite where I expected them to be. And I will be finding short black dog hairs forever.

When the last inspector had completed his last inspection, I walked around the basin to the Fremantle Sailing Club office where I was assigned a spot at the end of one of their five long piers. With the help of a man working on a nearby boat to cast off my bow line, I managed to power THE HAWKE OF TUONELA full throttle astern into the wind, swing around and get to the other dock, against which the good Doctor gleefully plastered me.

The 100-foot-long T end of the dock was empty and equipped for megayachts, with huge hard rubber fenders suspended horizontally by heavy chains. I managed to wedge my own fenders between HAWKE's topsides and the rubber, until near sunset when the Doctor weakened enough to enable me to reposition the boat properly with bow, stern and two spring lines at one end of the T, tripping over seagulls as I did.

Only a few seagulls were present when I arrived in the early afternoon, but the quantity of seagull droppings indicated that they were either extremely heavy eaters or they had friends. Many, many friends. Several hundred of whom showed up around 5:00 p.m. after a hard day at the office. Later I discovered that about half of them hung out during the day on a grassy patch near the dinghy launching ramp on the far side of the clubhouse, while the other half went to the fishing boat basin which is surrounded by restaurants where they extorted food from lunching tourists.

The end of A dock became the scene of a titanic struggle ending in a victory of which I am most proud.

By dark that first night the entire dock, all 100 feet of it, was covered with seagulls, wing to wing, beak to beak, feather to feather, squawking, shrieking, bickering, jostling for position, reminiscing about the good old days in Hollywood when they starred in a Hitchcock movie. After about an hour they had arranged themselves more or less to everyone's satisfaction and quieted down and went to sleep. Promptly at 4:00 a.m. they all awoke and cacophonously flew off to their day jobs.

I submitted to this for three days and nights, only chasing off those who dared land on THE HAWKE OF TUONELA's deck, but then a local man on a nearby boat gave me insight and hope. He brought a power washer down one afternoon and blasted most of the guano from the dock before setting out plastic owls to which he tied Mylar tape, which fluttered in the wind.

This worked only briefly. I watched as after about an hour

one brave and aggressive seagull mustered the courage to dart up and peck a fake owl, from which he tore a strip of Mylar. And the jig was up. The seagulls trooped back into the space they had temporarily vacated. But I devised a plan.

Each afternoon just before I walked up to take my shower, I hosed down my end of the T. The seagulls did not like the change and clustered at the other end. When they ventured forward again in the evening I threw pitchers of water at them. I also threw water at them whenever they woke me in the night.

Ultimately there was a tipping point to use the currently fashionable expression, and the night came when the seagulls stayed at their end of the dock and I slept happily at HAWKE's end. I didn't usually even have to throw water any longer. It was enough merely for me to poke my head out of the companionway and say, "Be gone!" to fill the air with a black and white feathered screeching cloud. The unfamiliar sense of power was enormous.

The dividing line at the far reach of my hose was as distinct as The Great Wall of China, and more unbreachable. At least until I left. I expect that it took the gulls all of two or three days to reclaim their lost territory.

The human residents of Fremantle and Perth were as friendly as the seagulls were not. I don't recall ever being any place where as many people came by either on foot or boat to ask how I was, how the passage had been, if I needed anything, if they could be of help. I don't recall ever receiving more invitations to people's homes.

In fact I didn't need much of anything that was not readily at hand. Fremantle is small, only about 25,000 people, and the harbor compact. Boat suppliers and repairers are almost all located immediately around the small craft basin, and the public transportation system is unparalled. A shuttle bus runs right by the club every ten minutes on a figure 8 route through the center of town, which is only a mile away. If necessary commuter trains can be caught there every fifteen minutes which reach downtown Perth in a half an hour and for less than $2 U.S. I can't recall any other place as convenient.

When I finally got the boat sorted and dried out—and I was still finding water in obscure lockers two weeks after my arrival—I realized that despite the severity of the passage, THE HAWKE OF TUONELA had not sustained any serious damage. We didn't need to haul out. Mostly it was wear and tear, minor breakage, and electronics.

A carpenter made nine new teak slats to replace those broken during the knockdown; a diesel mechanic replaced an engine overheating alarm that had been shorted out by too many waves in the cockpit; I rewired all the lights on the starboard side of the interior and the bilge pump; the jib was picked up by a sailmaker to redo several new patches I had glued on at sea; the chartplotter went to two electronics dealers before it was fixed. The cost of repairing the instrument system was so high that I decided to replace it, although not until after I reached Sydney. I still had depth readings.

I bought a new Windex for the masthead, but waited to have it installed until after Christmas, when Carol was going to fly out, bringing with her a new masthead light fitting and a new LED bulb, which hopefully would live more of its 100,000 hour expected life than had the last.

The day before Carol was due to arrive was like the day I made landfall, with clouds exploding into thunderstorms. Although only a few minutes of rain fell on the yacht basin, there were heavier showers nearby and impressive lightning and thunder close enough so that standing in the cockpit I felt the vibrations. According to the evening news, lightning strikes caused more than thirty bushfires around the city. I could see heavy smoke to the south.

For three weeks Carol and I were tourists. We went to restaurants, movies, took day trips on cruise boats on the Swan River, rented a car and drove around the southwest corner of the continent.

In Albany on the south coast I looked out on the Southern

Ocean at a white capped sea torn by gale force wind. Getting to Sydney might be interesting.

It soon seemed that Carol had never moved back to Boston. If she hadn't, we would have cruised slowly to Sydney with several stops. By myself I would stay at sea.

When she flew away in mid-January I feel vaguely uneasy, as though something was wrong.

26 Swan Song

THE HAWKE OF TUONELA's motion woke me at 1:00 a.m. It was smooth. After four days beating up the New South Wales coast against twenty-knot headwinds and an adverse current, too smooth.

At sunset I had tacked offshore just twenty-five miles south of Sydney Heads, intending to sail east until 2:00 then come about and be at the harbor entrance at 8:00 a.m. But the wind was still working a midnight shift, and going on deck at midnight to make a sail and/or course change had become routine. Put a reef in, take one out, set the main, drop it, furl or unfurl the jib, tack, jibe. And almost always exactly at midnight. With a first quarter moon setting early, I was having to replace the batteries in my headlamp every other night. Probably the wind had changed at midnight this night too and I was just so tired that I slept through it for a while.

I had slept dressed and so had only to slip on shoes and headlamp and switch on the GPS before going on deck. With most of the instrument system inoperative, I was using the chartplotter to check boat speed as well as position. The radar was already on in standby mode with a guard zone, making sweeps every ten minutes, though that had not done much good the night before when a ship made what seemed a dedicated attempt to run us down.

On deck the wind was very light and the sky, which had been overcast during the day, was now clear and starry. I unreefed the main and fully unfurled the jib and tacked, then went below to the chart table.

The chartplotter showed us twenty miles east of South Head,

making three knots. We'd still be at the harbor entrance not long after dawn. As I sat there, the radar began to beep. I checked the screen and saw two blips just within the six mile guard zone.

I stuck my head out and found the running lights, one set south of us, also heading in toward the bright loom of Sydney, the other off in darkness to the north. There went any chance of getting another hour or two of sleep.

As much as possible I stay away from shipping lanes, but early in the passage the wind had forced me close to Cape Leeuwin in West Australia and toward the end had kept me near shipping from Bass Strait on. Trying to beat around Cape Howe, the southeast corner of the continent, I had seen a steady procession of ships. Tacking inshore during the day and off-shore at night had kept us at a safe distance from most of them, but the radar alarm had awakened me on what I expected to be the penultimate night of this passage and my fourth circumnav-igation, but which almost became the last.

I turned off the alarm that night, then checked to see what had caused it. Waves often result in false alarms, but there was a definite blip to the northeast. I stuck my head around the dodger and saw its lights. My masthead tricolor was already on, and in moonlight THE HAWKE OF TUONELA's sails were clearly vis-ible. The ship was heading toward us. At three miles I decided it was going to pass too close, and came about and tacked away. I cannot be certain, but the ship appeared to alter course too, again turning toward us.

We were making six knots close-hauled, so I eased the sheets and turned father away from the ship onto a beam reach. Our speed increased to eight. Yet again the ship altered course to-ward us. I had the feeling that this was deliberate, that whoever was at the wheel was either through malevolence or boredom trying to run us down or at least see how close he could come, and there was no way I could outrun him.

I put the key in the engine ignition and turned it on. This would not increase our speed, but might enable us to maneuver at the last minute.

The ship loomed closer, filling the sky. I disengaged the Mon-

Closing the fourth circle. Just outside Sydney Heads

itor control lines and sat in the cockpit, tiller in hand. The sound of the ship's engine was distinct above the sounds of the sea. A loud throbbing rumble. I could feel vibrations through the water. And I could hear the hissing of the ship's bow wave as it passed a hundred feet off our stern, before the ship altered course back to the southwest, leaving us rolling wildly in its wake.

For an eerie moment the world fell silent. Time seemed to stop or maybe it was just my heart. Then sound and time resumed. Too close, I thought, and re-engaged the Monitor, hardened up the sails, and tacked back out to sea.

I went below and opened a can of Emu Bitter, a West Australian beer. By the time I had finished it the ship was outside the radar guard zone and I went back to sleep.

But for that incident, the three-week passage from Fremantle had been routine, with the three stretches I expected to be difficult passing easily.

Fremantle takes pride in claiming to be the third windiest

city in the world, after Chicago and Wellington, New Zealand. I left with a forecast of only twenty-knot headwinds and a cold front due in forty-eight hours.

This was another passage on which I welcomed cold fronts with their accompanying wind shifts to the west and south, favorable for THE HAWKE OF TUONELA heading east.

That first front arrived promptly on schedule, enabling us to pass Cape Leeuwin on a close reach.

The second area of concern was the Great Australian Bight, usually occupied by a big high during the southern summer. If necessary I was prepared to go back into the Forties, even as far as passing south of Tasmania. But while the wind made nightly shifts of at least 90°, it remained on or behind our beam, and THE HAWKE OF TUONELA sailed straight across the Bight.

The third was a thirty-mile wide stretch of Bass Strait from Wilson's Promontory, the southernmost point on the Australian mainland, to Flinders Island, off Tasmania, which is a slalom course of small islands, half-awash rocks, and strong currents. After being becalmed for a few hours the night before, I hit this in late afternoon with strong wind from astern, exactly where I wanted it, and with a single jibe was through by sunset.

At one point I found myself .8 of a nautical mile from one of those rocks, Crocodile Rock, presumably not named after the song, but an unlikely place for a crocodile nevertheless. The rock itself was invisible but marked by waves breaking in the middle of nowhere. In the old days of navigating by sextant—which is to say when I began making ocean passages thirty years ago—or at night, particularly if beating to windward, a sailor would have absolutely no warning.

The wind weakened as we eased toward Sydney on our last night at sea. After an hour the sails collapsed, filled, collapsed again, and I turned on the engine and furled the jib and lowered the main.

Although I was maintaining our usual passage fuel consumption of a thousand miles a gallon, I had powered for a few hours and knew that the prop was foul. I had forgotten to dive and clean it in Fremantle. We could only manage four knots under power, but that was enough. I didn't want to be there before dawn anyway, particularly this time.

The ships seemed to be waiting for dawn too. The one to the south remained abeam of us, while the one to the north made slow circles.

I recalled wondering when I sailed from Sydney in September 1991 if I would see the place again.

Now I was returning in February 2003 in what seemed to be a very slow circumnavigation, but could also be viewed as a two and a half year circumnavigation with a nine year intermission. Except for the thousand miles between Fort Lauderdale and Boston that I covered in May of 1995, the voyage was east from Sydney in September 1991 to New Zealand, around Cape Horn to Punta del Este, Rio de Janeiro, the Virgin Islands, and Fort Lauderdale which I reached in August 1992; and from Boston at the end of May 2001 to Portugal, Gibraltar, Senegal, Brazil, Cape Town, Fremantle, and now Sydney again in February 2003. As a

THE HAWKE OF TUONELA *at rest after the end of the fourth circumnavigation,* Elizabeth Bay, Sydney, Australia

goal it was purely existential, its only value created by the effort and sacrifice I was willing to make to accomplish it.

33°50′S 151°18′E was the first waypoint I put in the chart-plotter when I bought it three years earlier in Boston. And now 20,000 miles later it was the only one left.

The Australian continent frequently just comes to an abrupt halt and throws itself into the sea. The Nullabar Plain at the north end of the Great Australian Bight ends in hundreds of miles of the longest unbroken sea cliff in the world, and from seaward of Sydney there is little indication of what may well be the greatest natural harbor in the world. Captain Cook, who anchored in Botany Bay just to the south, passed without seeing anything worth investigating.

With the first gray light of dawn Sydney's pale concealing cliffs took shape through coastal clouds, then above them emerged the tops of high-rise buildings in the city center five miles up harbor.

A small powerboat with two men fishing moved across smooth pearly water, lifting on long swells. A green and tan ferryboat appeared from Manly to the north.

I cut the engine to just above idle and briefly ducked into the cabin to turn on the CD player.

We passed through Sydney Heads to the somber and serene notes of Jean Sibelius', "The Swan of Tuonela," which partially gave THE HAWKE OF TUONELA her name.

I patted the deck and said, "Hawkey, they're playing our song."

Other books of interest

A SINGLE WAVE
Stories of Storms and Survival
Webb Chiles
"Webb Chiles has been called 'sailing's best living writer and its worst lunatic.'
His book covers the dramatic highlights of 25 years in three boats.... Chiles is philosopher,
adventurer, confessor, seaman par excellence and, of course, survivor. Above all, he is a
consummate storyteller who, like a true pugilist, pulls no punches, but lands his
blows with the sensitivity of a poet." —*Yachting Monthly*

CAPE HORN
The Logical Route
Bernard Moitessier
This book is a mariner's guide to the pleasures and perils of sailing the trade winds, the
archipelagos of the Pacific, and the Cape Horn Route, including preparation suggestions and a
wealth of sailing survival knowledge that made the Moitessiers' voyage so successful and joyous.
"A true classic by and about one of cruising's best known authors."—*Latitudes & Attitudes*

FLIRTING WITH MERMAIDS
John Kretschmer
"Not only has John Kretschmer lived a life wildly festooned with adventure, romance, and
outrageous characters—his reality outstripping our most Walter Mittyesque sea fantasies—now
he has gone and turned it all into a collection of yarns that incite yet more envy among those of us
stuck behind landbound computers. Not only can the sailor sail—through hurricanes and civil
wars—but the sailor can write. It's a hell of a read." —Fred Grimm, *Miami Herald*

CRUISING JAPAN TO NEW ZEALAND
The Voyage of the SEAQUEST
Tere Batham
"A wonderful cruising yarn with many surprising twists as the adventures and miles unfold. Tere
Batham is both a born sailor and a born storyteller, and in the rarely traveled waters of Japan and
Micronesia, she found a fine place to indulge both passions."—Herb McCormick, *Cruising World*

SEASONED BY SALT
A Voyage in Search of the Caribbean
Jerry Mashaw and Anne MacClintock
Mashaw and MacClintock are not your average sailors. Their story brims with humor
and high adventure and reflects a deep respect for and understanding of the history,
people, and economy of the many Caribbean islands that they visit.
"...captures the feel of sailing among the Caribbean islands and realizing
what matters in life."—Daniel Hays

Sheridan House
America's Favorite Sailing Books
www.sheridanhouse.com